FREEDOM
from your
INNER CRITIC

FREEDOM
from your
INNER CRITIC

A Self-Therapy Approach

Jay Earley, PhD
Bonnie Weiss, LCSW

sounds true
BOULDER, COLORADO

Sounds True, Inc.
Boulder, CO 80306

This work is solely for personal growth and education. It should not be treated as a substitute
for professional assistance, therapeutic activities such as psychotherapy or counseling, or medical
advice. In the event of physical or mental distress, please consult with appropriate health
professionals. The application of protocols and information in this book is the choice of each
reader, who assumes full responsibility for his or her understandings, interpretations, and results.
The author and publisher assume no responsibility for the actions or choices of any reader.

Published 2013

Cover design by Jennifer Miles

Cover photo © Shutterstock.com

Printed in the United States of America

Library of Congress Cataloging-in-Publication Data
Earley, Jay, 1944-
  Freedom from your inner critic : a self-therapy approach / Jay Earley, PhD, and Bonnie Weiss, LCSW.
    pages cm
  ISBN 978-1-60407-942-5
  1. Criticism, Personal. 2. Self-acceptance. 3. Self. 4. Self-talk. I. Weiss, Bonnie. II. Title.
  BF637.C74E17 2013
  158.1--dc23

                        2013005623

Ebook ISBN: 978-1-62203-064-4

10 9 8 7 6 5 4 3 2 1

CONTENTS

CONTENTS

INTRODUCTION

People are like stained-glass windows: They sparkle and shine
when the sun is out. But when the darkness sets in, their true
beauty is revealed only if there is a light from within.

ELIZABETH KÜBLER-ROSS

Jeanette had a bad case of low self-esteem. When she was a child, all her teachers were puzzled by this. She was smart and musically gifted but had absolutely no confidence. She never auditioned for the orchestra or for school plays, even when she was encouraged to do so. As she got older, she ended up holding minimal jobs that didn't come close to tapping her native talents. She just assumed that she wouldn't amount to anything. Every time she had an inclination to reach out and try something challenging, she experienced a sinking feeling in her chest, and a gray cloud descended on her, leading her to give up on the idea.

One afternoon Jeanette's friend Lynn was having a very bad day; she complained to Jeanette of heaviness in her heart, about a critical voice that she heard inside of her. Suddenly something clicked with Jeanette; she recognized the voice her friend was describing. It lived inside her, too! It was saying critical things like, "You aren't any good. You can't do it. Don't even try." She had always just assumed that this was *the truth* about her. She had never viewed these harmful messages as coming from a separate part of her psyche. She recalled how she longed to try out for high school musicals, but this other voice spoke so forcefully that she didn't dare.

Jeannette had just met her *Inner Critic.*

Like Jeannette, many of us go through periods of believing there is something inherently wrong with us. When we explore inside, we too discover an Inner Critic. This part of us is responsible for our feelings of worthlessness. When we feel ashamed, hopeless, inadequate, or just plain awful about ourselves, it's because our Inner Critic is attacking us. When we believe its words, we often feel worthless, ashamed, or depressed. Inner Critic attacks can also lead to performance fears, writer's block, self-doubt, low self-esteem, guilt, obsessive thinking, or addictions.

Since the Inner Critic is one of the most difficult and tenacious issues that people face, we have collaborated on a serious study of how to work with and transform it. This book shows you how to address your Inner Critic using a powerful form of therapy: Internal Family Systems Therapy (IFS). Developed by Richard C. Schwartz, PhD, this cutting-edge form of psychotherapy has been spreading rapidly across the country since 2000. IFS can help you transform your Inner Critic into an inner resource that supports and helps you.

When Jeanette started IFS therapy with Bonnie, exploring her psyche and gradually getting to know her Inner Critic, she discovered, to her amazement, that this part was actually trying to *help* her. Its attacks were really distorted attempts to protect her. It wanted to keep her safe from failure and humiliation, and it figured that the best way to do so was to prevent her from ever trying anything difficult. It accomplished this by constantly judging and discouraging her.

Once Jeanette realized her Inner Critic's positive intent, she was no longer angry at it. She began to understand it and treat it more kindly. As she developed a friendlier attitude toward her Inner Critic, it became more reasonable and was willing to let her in to dialogue with it.

Exploring further, Jeanette discovered another part of her: a young-child part who received the Inner Critic's negative messages, believed its judgments, and felt worthless, defeated, and hopeless. We call this part the *Criticized Child.* Jeanette learned that she could also relate to *this* part of her and befriend it from a place of love and compassion. Using the IFS process, she accessed childhood memories about the origin of her Criticized Child—memories of being judged and dismissed and made to feel worthless. Jeanette then healed her Criticized Child through her love and helped it to release its feelings of shame and worthlessness. Her Inner Critic then receded into the background and caused less trouble in her life.

In addition, Jeanette discovered a helpful aspect of herself, one that we call the *Inner Champion,* which has the capacity to support and encourage us in the face of Inner Critic attacks. Jeanette's caring Inner Champion told her that she had a lot of talent and could accomplish great things in the world. She was able to develop and strengthen this Inner Champion and learned to evoke it when necessary and take in its support.

Her Inner Champion said, "You are OK just the way you are. You can do it. I'm proud of you." Hearing these messages helped Jeanette to take the risk to develop her musical talent and go to auditions. At long last, she moved ahead professionally in a career that she really loved. As her Inner Champion took over from her Inner Critic, she became happier and self-confident enough to pursue her dreams.

You too can put an end to your painful feelings and grow into the person you've always dreamed of being. The best part is that you can do it on your own using IFS.[1] Because it is so user-friendly, IFS lends itself especially well to self-therapy. We'll show how to use the IFS process to reweave your internal landscape.

First, in chapter 1, you'll understand how the Inner Critic works and discover which of the seven types of Inner Critics may be affecting you. In chapter 2, we will show you why your Critic isn't as powerful as it seems to be and how it is actually trying to help and protect you. With this essential background knowledge, we will lead you through the IFS process step by step in chapters 3 through 11. You'll learn how to use these steps to transform your Inner Critic into an Inner Champion and an Inner Mentor. We explain the relevant IFS concepts and procedures as we go, so you will be able to use it successfully even if you have no previous knowledge of IFS.

Criticism is a major factor in relationships, and many interpersonal problems are affected by the Inner Critic. In chapter 12, we will explore what happens when our criticism is directed at someone else and how our parts react when someone criticizes us. In chapters 13 and 14, we will apply what we have been learning to two common Inner Critic issues: perfectionism and addictions. In chapter 15, we discuss how changes in attitudes about gender have affected the content of Inner Critic attacks.

Throughout the book, you will find exercises that engage you on all levels during this transformative journey. We frequently pose questions to you that you can answer in a journal. By keeping a journal of the process, in addition to deepening the journey you will have a record to refer to for contemplation, encouragement, and even more clarifying insight.

You aren't stuck with the anguish and difficulties that stem from your Inner Critic. Your inner world *can* change. You can feel confident and capable and allow your life's journey to unfold in an exciting, self-directed way. It's time for your suffering to end.

The adage "you can love yourself" is not just a platitude. You deserve to feel good about yourself without having to earn it. Our self-therapy approach will help you to recognize your intrinsic self-worth and develop your self-confidence. By going through this process, you will reconnect with yourself—the self that isn't occluded by the Inner Critic's negative messages. You will discover the freedom that comes from being who you truly are, rather than trying to fit into the box your Inner Critic creates for you, so you can create a life of joy, confidence, and achievement. Vibrant self-esteem is your birthright; you needn't settle for anything less.

1

GETTING TO KNOW YOUR
INNER CRITIC

The world is nothing but my perception of it. I see only through
myself. I hear only through the filter of my story.

BYRON KATIE

When you feel ashamed, hopeless, inadequate, or just plain awful
about yourself, it's because your Inner Critic is attacking you. The
Inner Critic does this in a variety of ways, but most commonly, it
works by hammering you with negative messages about your self-worth. It may
criticize your looks, your work habits, your intelligence, the way you care for
others, or any number of other things. It may:

- Evaluate and judge your feelings and behavior and sometimes your core self.
- Tell you what you should and shouldn't do.
- Criticize you for not meeting its expectations or the expectations of
  people who are important to you.
- Doubt you and tell you that you can't be successful.
- Shame you for who you are.
- Make you feel guilty about things you have done.

Most people have a number of self-judging Inner Critic parts. For example, you might have one Critic that attacks you for how you overeat and how much you weigh, and another Critic that tells you that you're lazy and should be working harder.

THE SEVEN TYPES OF INNER CRITICS

We have identified seven specific types of Critics:

- The Perfectionist
- The Inner Controller
- The Taskmaster
- The Underminer
- The Destroyer
- The Guilt Tripper
- The Molder

Each type of Critic has a different motivation and strategy, and identifying which Critics are affecting you can be useful.

The Perfectionist tries to get you to do everything perfectly. It has very high standards for behavior, performance, and production. When you don't meet its standards, the Perfectionist attacks you by saying that your work or behavior isn't good enough, which makes it hard to finish projects. Sometimes the Perfectionist even makes it difficult to get started, as with writer's block. Our clients with Perfectionist Critics have pictured them in a variety of ways—a crab with pincers, a schoolmarm with super-high standards, a magnifying glass, and an inspector, especially El Exigente, "the demanding one," from a 1970s coffee commercial.

The Inner Controller tries to control impulsive behavior, such as overeating, getting enraged, using drugs, or engaging in other indulgent behavior. It shames you after you binge, use, or react with rage. It is usually in a constant battle with an impulsive part of you. Our clients with Inner Controllers have viewed them as a bulldog, a lion tamer, an angry guard, and a shaming mother.

The Taskmaster tries to get you to work hard in order to be successful. It attempts to motivate you by telling you that you're lazy, stupid, or incompetent. It often gets into a battle with another part that procrastinates as a way of avoiding work. The Taskmaster might be envisioned as a demanding foreman, a vigilant watchdog, a boot in the center of your back, or someone constantly keeping a bunch of plates spinning.

The Underminer tries to undermine your self-confidence and self-esteem so you won't take risks that might end in failure. It tells you that you are worthless and inadequate and that you'll never amount to anything. It may also try to prevent you from getting too big, powerful, or visible in order to avoid the threat of attack and rejection. (Remember Jeannette, Bonnie's client described in the introduction? Her Inner Critic was an Underminer.) The experience of being undermined can feel like a rug has been pulled out from under you or like you're walking on a treadmill where you work and sweat but go nowhere. It can also feel like you have a rope tied to your middle so you can't go forward or like you've come up against a glass wall.

The Destroyer attacks your fundamental self-worth. It is deeply shaming and tells you that you shouldn't exist. You might experience the Destroyer as a crushing force that wipes out your vitality or a pervasive negative energy that stamps out any sign of creativity, spontaneity, or desire. It might look like Darth Vader, a giant spider, a leech on the back of the neck, or an elephant crushing you underfoot.

The Guilt Tripper attacks you for a specific action you took (or didn't take) in the past that was harmful to someone, especially someone you care about. This Critic might also attack you for violating a deeply held value. It constantly makes you feel bad and will never forgive you. It might also make you feel guilty for repeated behaviors that it considers unacceptable in an attempt to get you to stop. Images of the Guilt Tripper from our clients include a nun, a judge, a despot exiling someone, a black cloud descending, and a weight on the shoulders. It can make you feel oozy and icky, heavy in the chest, or as if you are being smashed with a huge hammer.

The Molder tries to get you to fit a certain societal mold or act in a certain way that is based on your family or cultural mores. This mold can be any kind: caring, aggressive, outgoing, intellectual, or polite. This Critic attacks you when you don't fit into that mold and praises you when you do. Images for the Molder include a prison guard, a cage, a straightjacket, and a large rulebook, like a holy text, that determines what you should do at every moment.

RECOGNIZING YOUR INNER CRITICS

Let's look at some common examples of the ways Inner Critic messages manifest in our lives. You may recognize yourself and your Inner Critic in some of the following scenarios.

Jill had an important date planned with someone she really liked. The night before the date, she started to feel nervous, ran to the fridge, and binged on chocolate cake. Right after she wiped away the crumbs, she looked in the mirror and heard her Critic, an Inner Controller, say, "You look fat! No man will ever marry you!" She suddenly felt uglier than she ever had in her life. She worried furiously about how she was going to look on her date, even though it was still twenty-four hours away. When the time for the date finally arrived, she was so nervous and agitated that she could barely communicate. She was less like her authentic self and ended up sabotaging her chances of making a good impression.

Charlie was sitting in front of his computer, halfway through an important project, when his Inner Critic showed up. It told him that the work he'd done so far was garbage and then made him check and recheck it, wasting his precious time. Under this pressure, he couldn't get the rest of the project done on time. If his Inner Critic, a Perfectionist, hadn't derailed his work in this way, Charlie might have done a stellar job and gotten kudos from his boss.

Jennifer's ten-year-old son, Sean, was not meeting academic standards, but Jennifer felt as though she herself was failing. She had a job outside of the house and believed that her inability to spend every afternoon with Sean was at the root of his problems at school. When he brought home his report card, Jennifer acted outwardly nurturing and caring, but on the inside she was crying, thinking it was her fault. Her Guilt Tripper Critic said, "It's your fault! You haven't helped him enough."

YOUR CRITICS ARE UNIQUE

Even though we are using these seven categories of Critics, each Inner Critic of yours is unique with its own particular characteristics. For example, your Perfectionist won't be the same as anyone else's, or you might have one Critic that has characteristics of both a Molder and Guilt Tripper. Don't pigeonhole your Critics according to our descriptions of these categories. Discover your own Critics and their unique attributes.

Feel free to call your Critics by whatever names seem right; don't feel as though you must use *the Taskmaster* or *the Underminer*. As you'll see in chapter 5, one of our clients, George, called his Inner Critic *the Slave Driver*. One of Jay's clients, Sarah, whom you'll meet in the next chapter, called her Critic *the Attacker*.

EXERCISE **WHICH CRITICS DO YOU HAVE?**

Think of a way that one of your Critic parts attacks you. In your journal, answer the following questions.

- Under what circumstances does it attack you?
- What does it say to you?
- Which of the seven types of Critics do you think it is?

Example

Here is how Jill might answer the questions for this exercise:

- Under what circumstances does one of your Critics attack you? *Whenever I eat too much.*
- What does it say to you? *You're a fat slob. No man will ever be interested in you. You should be ashamed of yourself for pigging out like that.*
- Which of these seven types of Critics do you think it is? *Inner Controller*

EXERCISE THE INNER CRITIC QUESTIONNAIRE

We have devised a questionnaire to help you determine which of the seven types of Critics are problems for you. It is short and easy, usually not taking more than five or six minutes.[1]

After reading each of the statements, write the number that corresponds to the following:

0 = Never   1 = Not often   2 = Occasionally   3 = Frequently   4 = Always

1. I feel like I am intrinsically flawed.
2. I set high standards for myself.
3. I feel terrible about myself when I get out of control.
4. I push myself to work very hard so I can achieve my goals.
5. When I think of trying something new and challenging, I give up before I begin.
6. I am ashamed of everything about myself.
7. I am troubled by something I have done that I cannot forgive myself for.
8. I know who I ought to be, and I'm hard on myself when I act differently.
9. I expend a great deal of effort trying to control my impulsive behavior.
10. My self-confidence is so low that I don't believe I can succeed at anything.
11. I attack myself when I make a mistake.
12. I have trouble holding onto a positive sense of myself.
13. I have a hard time feeling OK about myself when I'm not acting in accordance with my childhood programming.

14. There is no end to the things I have to do.
15. I do things to people that I feel terribly guilty for.
16. There are indulgent parts of me that take over and get me into trouble, and then I punish myself for it.
17. I believe that it is safer not to try than to fail.
18. I get anxious and self-critical when things don't come out just right.
19. I feel ashamed when I don't measure up to others' expectations.
20. I tell myself that, if I were a good person, I would take better care of people I care about.
21. At a deep level I feel like I don't have the right to exist.
22. I feel bad because I am too lazy to really make it in the world.
23. I feel really ashamed of some of my habits.
24. I spend much more time than is needed on a project in order to make it as good as possible.
25. I have a nagging feeling that I am bad.
26. I try really hard to overcome my tendency to avoid doing tasks.
27. I feel bad because I can't be what my family or culture expects of me.
28. I feel that I don't have what it takes to succeed.

Now fill in your numerical answers from above in the blanks below and add up each line to get a total score for each group of four questions. This gives you a numerical score from 0 to 16 for each of the seven types of Critics.

Questions 2 ___ + 11 ___ + 18 ___ + 24 ___ = ___ Perfectionist Score

Questions 3 ___ + 9 ___ + 16 ___ + 23 ___ = ___ Inner Controller Score

Questions 4 ___ + 14 ___ + 22 ___ + 26 ___ = ___ Taskmaster Score

Questions 5 ___ + 10 ___ + 17 ___ + 28 ___ = ___ Underminer Score

Questions 1 ___ + 6 ___ + 12 ___ + 21 ___ = ___ Destroyer Score

Questions 7 ___ + 15 ___ + 20 ___ + 25 ___ = ___ Guilt Tripper Score

Questions 8 ___ + 13 ___ + 19 ___ + 27 ___ = ___ Molder Score

If you scored 9 or higher for a Critic, there is a good chance that it is causing problems for you. Those for which you scored 7 or 8 might be problematic. Those with scores 7 or less are less likely to be troublesome.

2

A NEW VIEW OF THE INNER CRITIC

As we tune into the Inner Critic, we begin to perceive it as an alarm system that signals a call for help. Someone is dialing 911. Someone is alerting us to the possibility of pain, shame or abandonment. It is as though the Inner Critic cries, "Look out! Please help me because I can't handle the situation."

HAL AND SIDRA STONE
Embracing Your Inner Critic

W hen we become aware of how our Inner Critic is tearing us down and ruining our lives, we usually react to it in one of the following ways.

We might try to just ignore the Inner Critic's attacks and think positive thoughts about ourselves. While this is much better than simply believing our Critic, it won't solve the problem because we're not really dealing with the Critic. This tactic may work at times, but then our Critic will override our attempts to ignore it and may sneer at our positive thoughts. Or it may sneak up on us with subtle attacks that we don't even notice.

Another strategy is to try to convince the Critic that it is wrong and that we are really worthwhile, competent, smart, and so on. This is better than ignoring the Critic, but we're still giving away our power. The Critic may or may not be convinced. And even though we may win the argument at times, our Critic usually comes back with even more powerful attacks.

Another common strategy is to try to get rid of the Critic—to give it the old heave-ho. Unfortunately, this really isn't possible. We can't get rid of a part of our psyche any more than we can get rid of a part of our body. We won't be able to cast out or banish our Inner Critic forever. It might go underground for a while, but it will pop up later and cause us even more grief.

IFS offers a larger understanding that these strategies miss. It recognizes that our psyches are made up of different *parts,* sometimes called *subpersonalities.* You can think of them as little people inside you. Each has its own perspective, feelings, memories, goals, and motivations. And because they do, these parts are often in conflict with one another. For example, one part of you might be trying to lose weight, and another part might want to eat a lot. But *all* our parts, including the Inner Critic, are trying to help us. When we accept and work with all our parts, none are demonized, and all can contribute to our wholeness and highest potential.

YOUR CRITIC'S POSITIVE INTENT

One of the most startling discoveries about our Inner Critics is that they are actually trying to help us. This is an amazing, powerful secret. In its own distorted, confused way, your Inner Critic is actually trying to help you. At first this may seem surprising, but once you get to know your Critic in a deeper way, you'll come to understand why it is attacking you. It may be negative and harsh, but it is doing so in a distorted attempt to protect you from pain. As strange as it may seem, we have found this to be true over and over with hundreds of clients, and so have other IFS therapists.

Your Inner Critic thinks that pushing and judging you will protect you from hurt and pain. It thinks that if it can get you to be a certain way—perfect, successful, cautious, nice, slim, outgoing, intellectual, macho, and so on—then you won't be shamed or rejected, and you might even get approval from people who are important to you. It tries to get you to fit in by prescribing rules and then attacking you if you violate them. Even though attacking you actually backfires and causes you more suffering, your Inner Critic is doing what it thinks is best for you.

The good news is that because the Inner Critic actually has positive intentions, you don't have to fight with it or overcome it. You don't have to win a battle; you don't have to get rid of it. Instead, you can discover what it thinks it's doing for you and make a positive connection with it. You can offer it appreciation for its efforts, and it can begin to trust you. Knowing that your Critic's heart is in the right place makes it possible to create a cooperative relationship with it and transform it into a valuable resource. This relationship makes an enormous difference in your internal landscape and sets the stage for deeper healing.

DIFFERENT CRITICS, DIFFERENT MOTIVATIONS

All Inner Critics are, in their own way, trying to help you, and the different types of Critics have different motivations and means.

Protecting You from Judgment or Rejection

For some Critics, the primary goal is to protect you from being judged, ridiculed, rejected, attacked, or abandoned by people. A Perfectionist Critic might be afraid that if you aren't perfect, you will be judged or dismissed, so it tries to get you to be perfect in everything you produce—even the way you look and operate in the world. It attacks you whenever you aren't top notch in every way. A Taskmaster Critic might try to get you to work hard so you will be really successful, because it believes that if you fail at anything or are even just mediocre, you will be attacked or rejected. It is a slave driver that judges you unmercifully whenever you aren't working to maximum effort.

A Molder Critic might be afraid you are stepping outside the mold of what is acceptable—for example, by gaining weight, being angry, being needy or vulnerable, or being strong and visible. It might also be afraid of your being sexual, feminine, artistic, introverted, or emotional. The definition of what isn't acceptable varies from one Critic to another, but they all believe that if you violate these standards, you will be ridiculed and excluded by your family, friends, or a group that is important to you. So they attack and shame you whenever you do anything that strays from the mold.

Getting Approval

Some Critics are primarily trying to get approval, attention, or admiration from people who are important to you. Perfectionists and Taskmasters believe that if you are perfect or very successful, you will gain the attention you have always wanted. Molders believe that if you fit the mold of just who your parents or culture expect you to be—outgoing, intellectual, caring, beautiful, dutiful, or whatever is most valued—then you will finally get the love you so desperately need. They may want you to get approval from your boss or your boyfriend, but their need for approval from these people actually stems from a need for approval from your parents or childhood friends.

These Critics push you to be a certain way, and they may even reward you when you succeed. But they certainly attack you when you don't succeed.

Jay writes: When I was struggling with my Critics, one of them judged me for being shy and introverted, which I was. Its judgments were accurate but not very helpful. When I would hang back at a party and avoid reaching out to women I was interested in, my Critic would tell me I was a loser who would never find love. If a woman rejected me, it attacked me even more strongly by telling me there was something wrong with me that made me unappealing to women. It was actually trying to motivate me to change—to become more outgoing, funny, confident, and so on—so I would attract women and find love. But its judgments had the opposite effect; they made me feel bad about myself and less likely to take social risks.

Preventing Damage

Some Critics try to stop you from doing things that are harmful to yourself or others. An Inner Controller Critic might want to keep you from overeating or abusing drugs, or perhaps to stop you from flying into a rage or acting impulsively. A Guilt Tripper Critic might want to stop you from doing anything that causes another person pain, such as forgetting someone's birthday or inadvertently saying something hurtful. If you do something like this, it attacks and shames you to try to keep you from doing it again.

Keeping You Safe from Attack

An Underminer Critic may be afraid that if you are powerful or confident, you might put yourself out in the world. You might take risks such as writing an article, asking a woman for a date, or speaking up at work. This Critic is afraid that taking these actions will put you in harm's way. So it criticizes you to keep you scared and small so you will be safe. It wants to make you submissive so you won't assert yourself and put yourself in danger. When someone attacks you, a Destroyer Critic might blame you for it in an attempt to get you to change yourself rather than standing up to the person and triggering more attacks. For example, if your supervisor at work dismisses your ideas, your Critic will say it was your fault rather than seeing that he was overloaded with work and not paying attention. This self-blame also allows you to stay attached to the person, your supervisor, so you won't be alone. Even though the focus may be on current life relationships, the Critic's motivation ultimately goes back to keeping you safe and connected to your parents.

Keeping You From Being Like a Parent

If you had a parent who didn't take care of you very well, or seriously harmed you, your Critic may feel extremely judgmental of that parent. It will also judge you harshly if you appear to be at all like that parent. Suppose you had a parent who was forgetful and disorganized, which resulted in your being neglected and abandoned. Your Critic may push you to be super responsible and attack you if you lapse at all, because the Critic is reminded of your parent when you do. Or if you had a parent who flew into rages and hit you, your Critic might judge you for feeling any anger or annoyance at all. The same may also happen if you were very embarrassed by one of your parents. If your father was a drunken slob at times and embarrassed you in front of your friends, you might have a Critic that attacks you for drinking any alcohol at all, or it requires you to be extremely neat in your appearance.

THE INNER CRITIC AS ENFORCER

One of the main reasons our Inner Critic parts judge us is to enforce a certain way of being—perfect, hardworking, moderate, or cautious, for example. If a Taskmaster Critic thinks it is important for you to always have your nose to the proverbial grindstone, it will push you to overwork and attack you when you don't. However, if you are generally a conscientious, focused worker, then there is no need for a Taskmaster Critic. You might very well have a part of you that works very hard, perhaps even too hard, but it wouldn't be a Critic; it would be just a hardworking part.

Jay writes: This has been the case with me. I have two hardworking parts, which I call *the Achiever* and *the Accomplisher.* The Achiever wants me to be highly successful professionally and tends to work very hard to get there, in a way that hasn't always been good for me. It isn't a Critic, however, because it has never judged me or pushed me. It just works hard. My Accomplisher is similar. It is ruled by my to-do list and gets completely caught up in getting things done, so that it can become like a machine with little presence or pleasure. But it isn't a Critic. It doesn't tell me to get things done. It just does them. I have worked on these parts for years, and now they have relaxed quite a bit. I am no longer driven to strive and can work with ease, which allows me a great deal of joy.

If you have a part that follows the rules, there is no need for the Critic to enforce them. For example, if you have a Dieter part that is very careful about the food you eat, there would be no need for an Inner Controller Critic to attack you. The Dieter might be overly rigid, but if it doesn't *judge* your eating, it's not a Critic.

This distinction highlights a very interesting characteristic of Inner Critic parts: *they have no power to act.* Therefore, they must judge us and push us in an attempt to enforce the way they want us to act. If they had the power to act, they would just do it; they wouldn't have to criticize us. Isn't it interesting that the Inner Critics we think are so powerful actually can't take action in the world? They certainly have the power to hurt us, and consequently they seem very powerful. But their judgments derive from their lack of power—from their frustration at not being able to act and their difficulty in getting us to act the way they want.

Because of the enforcer nature of Critics, one might suddenly judge you when you make a change in your life. Suppose you have been very careful about food all your adult life and have therefore never gotten any flak about your eating from a Critic. Lately you have been working on loosening up in some areas where you have felt restricted and are beginning to experiment with being more relaxed and less rigid about food. You might begin to be attacked by an Inner Controller Critic about this. Up until now, it didn't need to judge you because you were behaving in the way it wanted. Now that you are changing, it has become activated in order to enforce its view of how you should be.

THE INNER CRITIC ISN'T AS POWERFUL
AND FRIGHTENING AS IT SEEMS

Many Inner Critic parts think they must be powerful and scary to do their jobs. They think they must dominate you and be in control of you to protect you, so they act tough and project power. But these parts are actually not as confident as they seem; they are scared about what might happen if they didn't do their job. Recall in *The Wizard of Oz* when Dorothy and her friends went to see the wizard, the Great and Terrible Oz, they saw a variety of images that were formidable and frightening. However, these images were all just projected by a little man behind a screen to make himself seem powerful. He didn't actually have any magical powers at all. That is the way it often is with our Inner Critics. They are projections on the screens of our minds.

Many Inner Critics are actually child parts that took on the burden of protecting you when you were young. You may have been in a family situation where you were judged, harmed, or rejected, so a child part felt that something had to be done to protect you. This part believed that the only way to protect you was to judge you, in an effort to shape you into becoming what your family wanted. It thought judging was the way to stop you from being hurt, so it puffed itself up and began to attack you. This part wasn't innately a nasty Critic. It started out with more noble characteristics—such as clarity, strength, assertiveness, or energy—before it took on this judgmental role. When it is able to let go of its attacking strategy, it can regain its natural healthy role in your psyche.

Sarah, a member of one of Jay's groups, learned firsthand how a child part can develop into Inner Critic. By understanding her Critic's history and true motivation, she was able to begin to work constructively with it.

Sarah was very frightened of her Inner Critic. It screamed and yelled at her and crushed her with its powerful attacks. It told her that she was worthless and would never amount to anything. She called her Critic *the Attacker* and visualized it as a huge monster that was attacking her physically; it had great muscles and a loud voice.

Once she became openly interested in getting to know the Attacker, she discovered its positive intent. Here is what the Attacker said to her:

> Attacking is a game in our family. They're all doing it, so I've got to do it, too, and I've got to be good at it. If they're going to do that to me, then I'm going to do it to myself so they can't do it to me worse. This gives me the power of not being hurt by them. I'm trying to protect this child part from being hurt by them and from feeling all that hate and criticism from the family. That's too painful, so if I hurt her (the child part) instead, it won't be so bad because I'm the one hurting her—not the people whose love she really wants.

When a Critic is trying to protect us, it is really trying to protect one of our wounded inner child parts. In IFS, these parts are called *exiles* because they are usually pushed out of consciousness to keep us from feeling their pain.

Notice that Sarah's Attacker was actually hurting the very exile it was trying to protect. This is not unusual for Critics. In IFS, we call the exile that the Critic is trying to protect the *Protected Child.* The exile who believes the judgments of the Inner Critic and feels ashamed, worthless, not valuable, guilty, self-doubting, or inadequate is called the *Criticized Child.* In Sarah's case, the Protected Child and the Criticized Child were one and the same.

After hearing the Attacker explain its motivation, Sarah's view of it gradually changed. And the Attacker itself also changed. It became visibly smaller, less threatening, and more reasonable.

> Sarah: It's very competitive. The whole of my family is very competitive. The Attacker is doing two things: it's protecting me from them, but it also wants to be the best. It's really sad that it has to do that to protect me from the family. I feel compassion for the Attacker that it had to do that.

> Jay: So let the Attacker know of your compassion for it in some way. And see how it's responding to you.

Showing compassion helped to build the relationship between Sarah and the Attacker. Befriending your Critic in this way is a key step in the IFS process, one we'll guide you through in chapter 5.

S: It's having trouble taking that in.

J: Ask what the trouble is. What makes it hard for the Attacker to take that in?

S: Because it's so caught up in having to fight to survive . . . and to be heard.

J: So it's afraid that taking in your compassion will take the fight out of it?

S: Yeah, otherwise it'd get crushed by everyone in the family. It had to defend me. That's why it attacks so much—because everybody else was better at attacking. Maybe it attacked my brother sometimes, but it certainly couldn't attack my mom or dad.

J: I see. So it ended up attacking you because it could do that.

S: Yeah. But it did that to protect me from them. "I'll do it to myself so they don't hurt me." That's what it was about. "Anything you do can't get to me because I've hurt myself first."

J: It sounds as if you really understand where the Attacker got that strategy from.

S: It's crazy, isn't it? But it made sense at the time; it's all that part could do.

J: Let it know that you really understand where it was coming from.

S: OK.

J: Check and see how the Attacker is responding to you now.

S: It's calming down a bit.

J: See if there's anything more the Attacker wants to show you about what happened to make it take on this role.

S: We've pretty much got it. It thanks you for being patient enough to let it get this out.

The Attacker now seemed to trust Sarah and me, so I asked her to see if the Attacker would give us permission to heal the exile it was protecting. In IFS, we always ask permission from a protector before trying to work with the exile it is protecting.

When she asked for its permission, the Attacker told Sarah it felt scared.

J: Ask it what it's scared of.

S: That this Scared Kid would have to feel all that hate and criticism from the family. It's trying to protect that exile; it doesn't want the Scared Kid to feel that pain.

The Scared Kid was Sarah's name for the exile that the Attacker was trying to protect. The Attacker didn't understand that this Scared Kid, the exile it was determined to protect from pain, was already in pain. The Kid had been holding that pain ever since Sarah was young. If the Attacker allowed us to contact the Scared Kid, Sarah might experience its pain directly, but the Scared Kid wouldn't be exposed to any new pain. I explained this to the Attacker.

S (laughing): We haven't done a very good job there—the Kid is already feeling the pain.

J: I know it did its best, but it couldn't really protect the Scared Kid entirely, so it is carrying those memories and that pain. We're not going to make the Scared Kid feel worse. We're just going to witness the feelings it's holding and find out where it is stuck in the past.

My goal was to get the Attacker to give us permission to work with the Scared Kid and heal it (a process we'll lead you through in chapters 6 and 7). However, to my surprise, the Attacker went in a different direction.

S: It's really, really sad that it failed because it tried so hard to protect the Scared Kid.

J: That is really sad. Let the Attacker know that if it gives you permission, we could actually heal the Scared Kid now, so it won't have to carry around this pain anymore.

S: It says, "It's hard to believe that you could do it when I couldn't do it. It's my job. I've got to be able to do it."

J: We're not going to try to protect the Scared Kid. We're going to heal it.

S: It's skeptical that you can do that because it's tried for so long.

J: I totally understand that. But you see, we have this really powerful method called IFS to help. That's why it's possible.

S: The Attacker doesn't like giving up. It has to be the one to do it. "It's got to be me. I've got to do it. I've got to be responsible for her."

J: Wow, this part really took on a heavy burden, being responsible for the Scared Kid.

All the Attacker's attacks were really attempts to protect this hurt exile. And it felt that it had to do this because there was no help or support from anyone.

S: Oh, yeah. There was nobody else to help so it never learned how to let anyone else help. I guess it feels ashamed that you could do it when it couldn't. The Attacker is saying, "Then that reconfirms how useless and pathetic I am."

J: Well, tell the Attacker that it basically took on an impossible job. No child could have done that.

S: "Yes, that right. Not against them; they're too strong. There are too many of them. And I'm just a kid, you know."

Notice how all the Attacker's statements were in the present tense. It was really stuck in the past and experiencing that time as if it were happening in the present.

S: "I now realize that I'm just this little kid, and I'm trying to protect this other kid."

J: That's right; that's why it was an impossible job.

S: It's been trying to be an adult for so long. To protect me from the adults, it had to take on an adult assignment. It had to grow really quickly. It didn't get to be a kid.

When I heard this sentiment, I had tears in my eyes. The Attacker was actually a child part that was intent on protecting another child part, the Scared Kid, from pain. This is so different from the way we usually think of our Critics. It was also moving for Sarah and made it easy for her to feel compassion and caring for the Attacker. She saw that the real Attacker had been revealed, like the little man behind the curtain in the *Wizard of Oz*. And Sarah's image of the Attacker morphed again. Now she saw it as a frightened girl who was doing her best to act tough to prevent a terrible tragedy.

EXERCISE **YOUR INNER CRITIC'S POSITIVE INTENT**

Choose an Inner Critic to focus on. Review what it says to you and which situations tend to trigger it. Take out your journal and respond to the following prompts.

- What type of Inner Critic is it most like? Look over the seven types of Critics from chapter 2 and guess or sense which one.
- What is the Critic's positive motivation for you? Look over the various motivations discussed in this chapter and see if you can sense what this Critic is trying to do for you.

Example

Here is how Sarah answered the questions for this exercise:

- What type of Inner Critic is it most like? *Destroyer*
- What is the Critic's positive motivation for you? Look over the various motivations . . . and see if you can sense what this Critic is trying to do for you. *Attack me before my family does so the attack doesn't hurt so much. Get a sense of power and not be crushed by being able to attack.*

Seeing our Inner Critic as an enemy is a natural response to it, and conventional therapy often encourages that perspective. Many therapeutic approaches to the Inner Critic view it as just an attacking bully or an enemy, and they try to have you get rid of it or overcome it. They miss the larger understanding that IFS offers: *all* our parts are trying to help us.

Another important thing to remember about parts is that they usually only know one way to act and react. This is because they come from our childhood, when our psyches were still developing and we were faced with dangerous situations that we were too young to handle well. Our parts did the best they could, often using strategies that were extreme and shortsighted. Parts are not necessarily flexible, rational, or mature. This is especially true in the case of the Inner Critic. All it knows how to do is judge, whether or not judging works.

When you realize that your Inner Critic is actually trying to help and protect you, in its own distorted way, it is much easier to have compassion for it and to connect with it, opening it up for transformation.

COMING INTO SELF

Unblending from Your Critic and Child

Healing takes courage, and we all have courage,
even if we have to dig a little to find it.

TORI AMOS

I t *is* possible to get to know our Inner Critic and connect with it. This strategy is far more effective than fighting with the Critic. It allows us to negotiate with it and get it to relax, so it will stop judging and pushing us so much. However, in order to do this, we must be both separate from the Critic and openly curious about it. In addition, we also must be separate from our Criticized Child, the wounded child part in us who is hurt by the Critic. This chapter shows you how to get to that place in yourself.

ACCESSING YOUR INNER CRITIC

In an IFS session, we don't just understand our parts intellectually; we go inside and connect with them *experientially*. We dialogue with them and develop a relationship with them. Therefore, to begin this process, you can access a part through feeling your body or your emotions, getting an image of what it looks like, or hearing its words. Most people access Inner Critic parts by listening to their attacking words and through images. For example, recall that Sarah's Critic said that she was worthless, and she had an image of it as a huge monster.

You can also access parts through your body and emotions. However, if you try to access an Inner Critic part that way, you are likely to feel your hurt, depression, or hopelessness, and you will sense how this feels in your body—perhaps your chest is collapsed, or there is a weight on your shoulders or pain in your heart. These sensations are coming from the Criticized Child, not the Critic. It is useful to access those feelings and sensations, but remember to work with the two parts separately. Many people mix them up at first, which can be confusing and make your work difficult. Occasionally, someone does access the Critic through feelings or sensations. For example, you might feel tightness in your neck and jaw and a feeling of contempt. That would be the somatic (bodily) experience of the Critic.

THE SELF

In order to take the next step in the process, you must understand the *Self*, one of the most important IFS concepts. IFS recognizes that underneath all of our parts, every human being has a true Self that is wise, deep, strong, and loving. This is who we truly are when we aren't being hijacked by the painful or defensive voices of our parts. With its compassion, curiosity, and connectedness, the Self is the key to healing and integrating our disparate parts. It is also the natural leader of our inner family, a guide through the adventures of life. IFS can help you access your Self, and from that place of groundedness and love, you can connect with your troubled parts and heal them.

Let's look at three qualities of the Self that are particularly important for psychological healing. When you are in Self, you will naturally embody these qualities.

> **The Self is connected.** When you are in Self, you naturally feel close to other people and want to relate in harmonious, supportive ways. You are drawn to make contact with them, to be in community. The Self also wants to be connected to your parts. When you are in Self, you are interested in having a relationship with each of your parts, including your Inner Critics, which helps them to trust you and opens the way for healing.
>
> **The Self is curious.** When you are in Self, you are curious about other people in an open, accepting way. When you ask what makes them tick, it's because you want to understand them, not judge them. The Self is also curious about the inner workings

of your mind. When you are in Self, you want to understand why each part acts as it does, what its positive intent is for you, and what it is trying to protect you from. This curiosity comes from an accepting place, not a critical one. When parts sense this genuine interest, they know they are entering a welcoming environment, and they aren't afraid to reveal themselves to you.

The Self is compassionate. Compassion is a form of kindness and love that arises when people are in pain. You genuinely care about how they feel and want to support them through difficult times. When you are in Self, you naturally feel compassion for others as well as yourself. Your extreme parts are reacting to pain; some feel it, and some try to avoid it. So compassion is really needed to hold, support, and nurture you while you take on very difficult material. When you are in Self, you feel compassion for your parts. They can sense this, and it makes them feel safe and cared for, so they want to open up and share themselves with you.

In IFS, you don't try to get to know your Critic (or any part) unless you are in Self, which means that you feel open to the Critic and want to understand it from its own point of view.

BLENDING: WHAT HAPPENS WHEN YOU'RE NOT IN SELF

Blending is another key concept in IFS. At any given moment, you are either in Self or a part is blended with Self. You are either feeling curious, open, and compassionate because you are in Self, or you have been taken over by a part and are engulfed in its feelings and beliefs. Whoever is in charge of your psyche at any given moment is in your *Seat of Consciousness.* The Self is the natural occupant of the Seat of Consciousness. However, if a part, such as the Inner Critic or the Criticized Child, blends with you, it takes over the Seat and determines how you feel and react.

When you are judging yourself, an Inner Critic part is blended with you and sitting in the Seat of Consciousness. When you are feeling bad about yourself, a Criticized Child part is blended with you and sitting in the Seat. Often both the Critic and the Criticized Child are blended with you at the same time, which means that they're both occupying the Seat of Consciousness, and the Self is pushed into the background.

You can only work successfully with an Inner Critic if you aren't blended with it or the Criticized Child. Imagine a situation in which a father repeatedly punishes a child in a harsh way. What can be done about this? The child can't do anything. She is too young and scared. She has no power or perspective. The father can't do anything because he believes he is right. He is caught up in his judgmental role. Only a third person can intervene and change things. In your internal world, *you* become that third person when you aren't being either the "father" (the Critic) or the child (the Criticized Child). To become that third person means you must unblend from them.

When you unblend in this way, it doesn't mean that the self-judgment disappears or you stop feeling bad about yourself. It just means that you aren't completely taken over by these feelings. You have some space inside that is separate from them. Your Self has regained the Seat of Consciousness, and the Critic and Child have moved aside. You don't fully buy into the idea that you are inadequate. You can see that this idea is just the result of a part attacking you rather than believing it is the truth about you. For example, when your Critic says that you are a loser and will never find love in your life, you recognize that this is an attack from this part of you. It may not be the truth.

Though you may still feel sad or ashamed, when you are unblended from the Critic and Criticized Child, you aren't dominated by these feelings. You have a place in you (Self) that is feeling solid and calm. From this place, you can view these feelings, understand these attacks, and work with them. Parts of you may feel hurt to hear the message that you are a loser and hopeless about your love life, but that isn't all that's going on. You reside in a place that is deeper than those emotions, a place of calmness and curiosity.

UNBLENDING FROM YOUR CRITIC

Unblending from the Critic and coming into Self is not the final solution to your Inner Critic problem. It is just a preliminary step that gives you enough space to work with your Inner Critic in a constructive way.

Feeling worthless is just the result of an Inner Critic attack and not necessarily the truth about you. Reminding yourself of this truth will go a long way toward helping you to unblend from the Critic. If this reminder isn't enough, there is more you can do.

One option is to visualize the Critic as separate from yourself. Allow a visual image of the Critic to arise. This will give you the sense of it as a separate entity. Now visualize that the Critic is clearly a certain distance away from you. The further away it is, the more separation there is between you and it.

Another way to accomplish visual separation is to draw or paint an image of the Critic. Or you can choose an object from your home, an image in a magazine, or a picture from the Internet that represents the Critic. Having a concrete token of the part helps to create separation.

You can also unblend from the Critic by looking around inside for a part of you that argues with the Critic or wants to get rid of it. (We call this part the Inner Defender, a concept we'll talk more about in chapters 4 and 11.) Listening to the messages of this other part will help you to separate from the Critic.

UNBLENDING FROM YOUR CRITICIZED CHILD

If you are scared of the Critic or feel crushed by it, or if you feel depressed, sad, hopeless, or worthless, remember that these feelings come from your Criticized Child, not from your Self.

Take a few moments to access a powerful, nurturing side of you (these are aspects of Self). Now focus on the sad, hopeless feelings, which are coming from the Criticized Child. Let it know that you understand its hurt and feel compassion for it. Give the Child some time to take in your caring. Then ask the Child if it would be willing to step aside into a safe place, where you will protect it from the Critic. Explain that you (as Self) will be connecting with the Critic and you won't allow the Critic to attack the Child. Having the Child step aside will allow you to get to know the Critic from the place of Self. This is what Sarah did to unblend from her Criticized Child, the Scared Kid, in her IFS session with Jay:

> Jay: Check to see how you're feeling toward the Attacker [the Critic] right now.
>
> Sarah: Well, I'm really scared of it.
>
> J: OK, that probably means that you're blended with the Scared Kid. So ask the Kid if it would be willing to step aside into a safe place. And let it know that we're going to work with the Attacker to understand it and connect with it. And we're not going to let it do more attacking. We're going to try to connect with it. See if the Scared Kid would be willing to step aside for you to do that.
>
> S: Yeah, so now it has stepped aside.

You can also create an experience of separation inside yourself so you feel your Self as different from the Child. You might experience this separation as moving back from the Child into a grounded place, or shifting into the stance of a witness, or moving deeper inside to a centered presence. Some people sense this shift as a stepping away from the Child *into* themselves. The following meditation is another way to help you access Self.

EXERCISE **SELF MEDITATION**

Let go of your focus on the Critic for a moment, and guide yourself in a meditation in which you become grounded and present in your body. If you are familiar with meditation, you can use whatever form works for you. If you aren't, you can use the following as a guide. Read the following paragraphs slowly, with many pauses. You could also ask a partner to read it to you.

Sit quietly with your spine relaxed but straight. Close your eyes and focus your attention on the sensations in your body. You might notice tension in your shoulders or pressure behind your closed eyes. There might be a sensation of warmth in your chest or fullness in your belly. Take your time and notice whatever body sensations come to your attention. These will probably change from moment to moment.

As you notice each sensation, take some time to feel it and be present with it in that moment. If you notice your attention wandering away from your body, gently bring it back, without judgment. Don't worry if your attention wanders more than once. Without judgment, bring your attention back to your body each time.

After a while, allow your attention to move down into your belly. Be aware of the sensations in your belly or just sense the physical presence of your belly. Relax into this sensation. Allow it to calm you and center you. Be with your belly for a while in a soft, open way. Allow your sense of yourself to deepen.

When you are located solidly in Self, end the meditation and return your attention to the Criticized Child. See if you now feel separate from it. Feel free to vary this meditation according to your preferences and your experience with similar guided meditations. Use what works for you.

WORKING FURTHER WITH THE CRITICIZED CHILD

If these methods of unblending from the Criticized Child don't work, you may need to spend some concentrated time with the Child. Let go of trying to work with the Critic for now, and take the time to get to know the Child and develop a relationship with it. As Self, ask the Child more about how it feels, and witness whatever it tells you or shows you. Don't try to change the Child; just listen to it with compassion in your heart, so that it feels safe and connected with you. This will make it much easier for the Child to unblend.[1]

EXERCISE UNBLENDING FROM THE INNER
CRITIC AND CRITICIZED CHILD

This exercise takes you through the steps described in this chapter. Use your journal to record your responses.

- Choose one situation in which one of your Inner Critics usually attacks you. Imagine that this situation is happening right now. What is your Inner Critic saying to you?
- Close your eyes and allow an image of the Inner Critic to emerge, or access your Critic through your body or feelings. What does your Critic look, sound, or feel like?
- If you feel judgmental toward yourself, then you are blended with the Inner Critic. See if you can unblend from it using the techniques described in this chapter. Take notes on how you did this. How were you able to create separation?
- If you are scared of this Inner Critic or feel crushed by it, those feelings are coming from the Criticized Child. What are these feelings?
- Check to see if you have an image of the Criticized Child. What does your Criticized Child look or feel like?
- In order to unblend from the Criticized Child, ask it to step aside into a safe place (maybe with a strong protector), or visualize the Critic in another room, or use the "Self Meditation" exercise to ground yourself. Take notes on how you did this.

You should now be separate from both the Critic and the Child. If you like, you can continue with "Unblending from the Inner Defender," the exercise in chapter 4.

Example

Here is how Sarah answered the questions in this exercise:

- Choose one situation in which one of your Inner Critics usually attacks you. Imagine that this situation is happening right now. What is your Inner Critic saying to you? *You're less than nothing. You don't deserve to even be here. Get lost!*
- Close your eyes and allow an image of the Inner Critic to emerge. Or access your Critic through your body or feelings. What does your Critic look, sound, or feel like? *A huge powerful monster with great muscles and a loud voice that is attacking me.*

- If you feel judgmental toward yourself, then you are blended with the Inner Critic. See if you can unblend from it using the techniques described in this chapter. Take notes on how you did this. *I visualized it as separate.*
- If you are scared of this Inner Critic or feel crushed by it, then those feelings are coming from the Criticized Child. What are these feelings? *Scared of it.*
- Check to see if you have an image of the Criticized Child. What does your Criticized Child look or feel like? *Battered and crushed.*
- Take notes on how you unblended from the Criticized Child: *I asked it to step into a safe room where a nurturing part cared for it.*

4

BECOMING OPEN TO YOUR CRITIC

Unblending from Your Inner Defender

I know quite certainly that I myself have no special talent;
curiosity, obsession and dogged endurance, combined
with self-criticism, have brought me to my ideas.

ALBERT EINSTEIN

Knowing that your Inner Critic part is trying to help you and protect you from pain means that you can connect with it and develop a cooperative, trusting relationship. This is the best way to help the Critic to relax and ultimately to transform.

A key IFS principle is that all parts are welcome. This means we need to be genuinely open to getting to know each part from a curious and compassionate place, which will encourage it to reveal itself. In order to do this, you must be in Self, which will allow you to be openly curious about the Critic and respectful of it. The Critic can tell if you feel negatively toward it, and it probably won't show you much about itself, but will just continue attacking you. Remember our earlier metaphor with the harsh father (Critic) and the hurt child. In order for change to occur, a third person (the Self) must intervene. But this person can only make a difference if the father trusts her. If he feels that she is judging him for the way he is treating his child, he won't give her the time of day. She must genuinely be interested in where he is coming from; then he might listen to her.

In this chapter, we will show you how to unblend from the *Inner Defender,* a part that prevents you from opening to the Inner Critic with the curiosity and compassion of the Self.

RECOGNIZING YOUR INNER DEFENDER

To check to see if you are in Self, notice how you feel toward your Inner Critic right now. Do you like it or hate it? Do you appreciate it or judge it? Do you want to banish it? Are you afraid of it? Are you curious about it?

The purpose of this inquiry is to discover whether you are in Self with respect to the Critic. Being genuinely open to your Inner Critic is not always easy. If it has been causing you pain, it is natural for you to be angry with it. It would be understandable if you judge it and want to be rid of it. However, approaching the Critic (or any part) with these attitudes won't lead to healing and reconciliation.

These attitudes aren't coming from your Self; they are coming from another part of you that we call the *Inner Defender,* because it wants to defend you from the Critic. Often the Inner Defender feels judgmental and angry toward the Critic. It may try to dismiss the Critic or even banish it from your psyche. But remember, you can't get rid of a part, and the Critic usually fights back successfully against attempts to dismiss it.[1]

Sometimes your Inner Defender tries to argue with the Inner Critic. If the Critic says that you are worthless, the Defender tries to prove that you are a good person who has accomplished things in your life. If the Critic says you can't succeed, the Defender argues that you can. If the Critic says you are a lazy bum who must work harder, the Defender may say, "Leave me alone." It wants to engage with the Critic and defend your goodness and your right to be yourself. It wants to fight against being controlled by the Critic. For example, Jay's client Sarah had a Defender that wanted to convince her Critic that she was a valuable person who could make it in the world. While it makes sense that your Inner Defender wants to champion you, engaging with the Critic in this way usually doesn't work. First, the Critic often wins the argument. Or if your Inner Defender wins for now, the Critic may redouble its attacks later. Second, this approach creates inner conflict.

UNBLENDING FROM YOUR INNER DEFENDER

If you realize that you are blended with the Inner Defender, ask that part if it would be willing to step aside so that you can get to know the Critic from an open place. Explain that doing this will help you to work successfully with the Critic to help it relax and transform. After all, the Inner Defender is probably not willing to step aside because it wants to fight or get rid of the Critic. Explain that the best way to resolve the pain the Critic is causing is to transform it.

You might first need to give the Defender some space to express its judgments and concerns about the Critic. Stop trying to get it to step back, and instead spend some time finding out about its role in your psyche. What does it do for you? It may have a larger role than just fighting against the Critic. Focus your attention on it for a while and get to know it. Give it time to explain itself to you. Make sure that it has had its say and feels that you understand it. Then once you understand it, give it appreciation for its efforts on your behalf. This should help you to develop a trusting relationship with it. Then it will probably be willing to step aside.[2]

If the Defender has expressed itself and still isn't willing to step aside, ask what it is afraid would happen if it did. Take some time to fully understand its fears and empathize with them. Defenders are usually afraid that if they give the Critic an inch, it will take over and attack you. Once you understand the Defender's fears, reassure it that you will handle the situation safely. Explain that you won't allow the Critic to take over—that you will be in Self and in charge while making a connection with it. The Critic won't be attacking because you will be asking it questions about its motivation, not listening to its judgments.

You might have more than one part that is an Inner Defender. One might argue with the Critic; another might rebel against it; a third might try to get rid of it.

At first Jay's client Sarah was angry at her Critic, the Attacker, and wanted to get rid of it because it caused her so much fear and pain. Clearly she wasn't in Self. She needed to get her Inner Defender, which she called the Blamer, to step aside so she could be open to the Attacker.[3]

Sarah: Now that the scared part has stepped aside, the Blamer comes out.

Jay: That part is blaming the Attacker?

S: Yeah, we don't like it. We don't like being criticized all the time . . . so a bit of a feeling of resentment toward the Critic comes out.

J: So ask the Blamer if it would be willing to step aside in order for you to work with the Attacker in a way that will help the Attacker to be less critical and to let go of its role.

S: It's amazing how strong that part is. It wants to get in there and fight the Attacker.

J: So maybe it needs to be heard a little more. Does the Blamer need to speak about its feelings toward the Attacker?

S: Yes. Coincidentally, just last week, I actually stood up to my mom for the first time ever. I really told her I was fed up with her criticizing my life. I'd never let the Blamer really tell her before, so it's in its power at the moment and wants to stay there.

J: That makes a lot of sense. It sounds as if it was a really good thing that the Blamer stood up to your mother.

S: Yeah, it really likes to tell her off—and tell the Attacker off. So how do I get it to step aside?

J: Well, you might explain to the Blamer that the Attacker is different from your mother. It may be modeled after your mother, but the Attacker is actually a part of you. It's actually trying to help you, in its own distorted way.

S: OK. It can begin to see that.

J: And see if the Blamer might be willing to step aside and let you connect with the Attacker and help it to let go.

S: Yup. That works.

J: So it's willing to step aside? Thank the Blamer for that. That's a big thing to do.

S: It was the way you put it. It made it easier.

Once Sarah was able to unblend from the Blamer, she could be open to her Inner Critic from Self.

THE VALUE OF BEING IN SELF

In IFS, you don't try to get to know your Critic (or any part) unless you are in Self, which means that you feel open to it and want to understand it from its own point of view. Once Sarah was able to unblend from the Blamer, she could be open to her Inner Critic from Self. This is the best place from which to be successful in working with the Critic.

When you are in Self, you are interested in knowing what makes the Critic tick, how it sees the world, and what it is *trying* to do for you. You can sympathize with the Critic's need to avoid pain and protect you from harm. This doesn't mean that you allow the Critic to keep attacking you. It doesn't mean that you believe its judgments of you. You stay in Self, where you are separate from the Critic and can see that it is causing you problems, but you are nevertheless open to getting to know it because you know its heart is in the right place. You are interested in connecting with it in order to ultimately transform it.

EXERCISE UNBLENDING FROM THE INNER DEFENDER

This exercise takes you through the steps as described in this chapter. Choose an Inner Critic that you want to work with. Then unblend from the Critic and the Criticized Child as described in the previous chapter. Remember that this Inner Critic is trying to help you and protect you. See if you can be open to learning about it from its perspective.

Now notice how you feel about your Critic. Do you like it or hate it? Do you appreciate it or judge it? Do you want to banish it? Are you afraid of it? Are you curious about it? Write about your feelings in your journal.

If you are angry at the Inner Critic or want to argue with it or get rid of it, you are blended with your Inner Defender.

- Name of Inner Defender:
- Ask that part what its concerns are:

Validate its concerns and then ask the Defender to step aside so you can be successful in working with the Critic. If it steps aside, check again to see how you are feeling toward the Critic and write this down.

Now you are finally in Self—openly curious about the Critic and interested in learning about it from its perspective. How do you feel toward the Critic now that you are in Self?

Ask the Critic to tell you or show you what it is trying to accomplish by judging you and write that down.

Example

Here is how Sarah, Jay's client, responded when she did the exercise:

- Name of Inner Defender: *The Blamer*

- Ask that part what its concerns are. *Doesn't like being criticized. Wants to get rid of the Attacker. If it stepped aside, the Attacker would really take over and make me miserable.*
- Validate its concerns and then ask the Defender to step aside so you can be successful in working with the Critic. How do you feel toward the Critic now that you are in Self? *Open and interested in what it is about.*
- Ask the Critic to tell you or show you what it is trying to accomplish by judging you. *Attack me before my family does so it doesn't hurt so much. Get a sense of power and not being crushed by being able to attack.*

5

BEFRIENDING YOUR INNER CRITIC

*The journey to discovery with my clients has led to astounding
conclusions about who we really are. Not only are we much more
at our core than we could imagine, the very aspects of us that
we thought proved our worthlessness are actually diamonds in
the rough. We are inherently good through and through.*

RICHARD C. SCHWARTZ
Introduction to the Internal Family Systems Model

Once you are in Self, the next step in your IFS session is to get to know your Inner Critic and develop a cooperative relationship with it. This relationship will provide the basis for further healing and transformation.

DISCOVERING YOUR CRITIC'S POSITIVE INTENT

The first thing you want to do is discover your Critic's positive intent—its motivation for attacking you. Your Inner Critic thinks attacking you will help you, so you can ask it some questions to find out its rationale. A good question to start with is, "What are you trying to accomplish by judging (or shaming or pushing) me?"

Make sure you are asking this question from genuine curiosity—not, "How could you possibly think this will help me, you stupid jerk?" Find the place inside you that is truly interested in finding out what this part is trying to do for you. Ask from that place.

Once the Critic answers the first motivation question, follow up with any questions that naturally come up for you. For example, if it says it is trying to get you to work harder, you might ask how it thinks judging you will make you work harder. Or you might ask what it hopes you will get by working harder. If you aren't sure why this part started judging you, you might ask what happened that made it decide that it was important to judge you.

Eventually, it is important to ask, "What are you afraid would happen if you didn't tell me I'm ugly?" (Or whatever it says to you.) The Critic's response often provides a deeper understanding of what it is trying to protect you from. Sarah, Jay's client, discovered that her Critic was trying to protect her Criticized Child from the attacks of her family, for example.

DEALING WITH A MISTRUSTFUL CRITIC

Sometimes a Critic will just respond with more criticism. Don't accept this. Critics are never just giving you information about how inadequate you are. They always have a reason. Continue to ask it to answer your question about its motivation.

Some Critics will say that they aren't trying to accomplish anything. "You are just a loser (or worthless, etc.), and I just want you to know that." Some may refuse to talk to you at all. All of these responses usually mean that the Critic doesn't really believe that you want to get to know it. It believes that you just want to overpower it or get rid of it. This belief isn't all that surprising, because there are probably parts of you that *do* want to get rid of it—namely your Inner Defender parts. In fact, often those parts have been quite actively trying to combat the Critic. It's no wonder the Critic isn't ready to trust you so fast.

Let's return to the metaphor of the harsh father, the child, and the third person. When you're not in Self, but are blended with another part of you that is working against the Critic, it's as if the third person (you) has been judging the father and telling him that he is treating his child badly. The father's response has been, "Get lost. She's my kid, and I'll treat her the way I want." When you suddenly switch to being genuinely interested, without judgment, in why the father is treating the child this way, it's not surprising that he might be taken aback and not immediately trust you.

If a Critic resists your questions, ask, "What are you afraid would happen if you did dialogue with me and answer my questions?" It will usually say, "You will try to stop me from doing my job," or "You will try to get rid of me." Reassure it that you aren't trying to do either of these things. In IFS, we never try to force a part to change or give up its job. And we never try to get rid of a part.

We are hoping that your Critic will relax and choose a new role in your internal system, but only if it wants to—never through coercion. We just want to get to know it, discover its motivation, and connect with it. Any further change will happen as the work develops, but only if the Critic chooses to change because it no longer feels a need to protect the exile in the same way.[1]

Jay writes: Here's how George, one of my clients, dealt with his mistrustful Inner Critic. Having accessed the Critic and unblended from his Criticized Child and Inner Defender, George was then in Self and ready to get to know the Critic.

Jay: Ask the Critic to tell you what it's trying to accomplish by judging you the way it does.

George: It's not letting me know. It just wants to start berating me again.

J: So ask it if it doesn't trust you or if it doesn't trust me.

G: It doesn't care.

J: So it just wants to berate you; it doesn't want to talk about what its role is. Is that right?

G: Yeah.

J: So ask it what it's afraid would happen if it answered that question and talked about its role. If it were willing to talk to you about the judgments, what is it afraid would happen?

G: That you'd make it go away.

J: OK, I can understand why it might think that. So explain to the Critic that we're not going to try to make it go away—that we never try to make any parts go away. We don't coerce them, and we're not trying to fight with them. We're actually interested in getting to know the Critic and making a connection with it.

G: It says, "I enjoy doing this job."

George's Critic was still not answering the question, so I asked in a different way in hopes that it would.

J: OK. So ask it what it's trying to accomplish by doing the job.

G: It says it is trying to get me to work hard and do well. I'm so lazy! I need to try harder.

It looked as if the Critic had accepted what I said and was trusting us enough to go on, because it began to answer the question about its motivation. So we could proceed to get to know it.

J: OK. The Critic is trying to motivate you to try to work more, is that right?

G: Yes. It wants me to be smart and please my boss, not let things go until the last minute and then do a poor job. I am going to call it *the Slave Driver*.

J: Ask it what it hopes you will get by working harder and pleasing your boss.

G: It wants him to like me and appreciate me. It wants me to get better assignments and to be put on more interesting jobs and teams. It wants me to get a raise.

J: It wants you to get approval and the benefits that accompany that.

G: Yeah. The real issue is that the Slave Driver wants my boss to think I'm really competent and smart.

J: And what does it hope that you will get from that?

G: I will get in with my boss . . . and I'll feel really good about myself. That's what it wants.

J: OK. That makes sense. I appreciate that goal. Ask the Slave Driver how it thinks that judging you will get you this. How will judging you get you to work harder?

G: Well, it figures that if it pushes me to work hard and judges me when I don't, then I will eventually get the message. I will buckle down and do good work.

J. Uh huh. I see that.

G: Although it is doubtful about my ability to really change. It says I'm hopeless.

J: Ask the Slave Driver what it is afraid would happen if it didn't push you and judge you.

G: It says, "Hah! It would be like now, only worse. You would just be lazy and avoid doing the work. You would really be a failure, and your boss would really look down on you—even worse than he does now. At least now, I get you to do some work. I keep you from being a complete deadbeat."

J: So the Slave Driver wants to protect you from being looked down on by your boss. And, of course, it really wants you to get his approval.

G: Yes, that's right. The Slave Driver says that you understand it.

J: Does that make sense to you, what the Slave Driver is trying to do for you?

G: Yes. I see it.

When George understood the Slave Driver's positive intent, and the Slave Driver saw that he did, we could move on to solidifying George's relationship with the Slave Driver.

DEVELOPING A TRUSTING RELATIONSHIP WITH YOUR CRITIC

Discovering the Critic's positive motivation isn't enough. It is also important to develop a relationship in which it trusts that you appreciate its efforts and roughly share its goals. Most of the time, the Critic has a faulty and damaging strategy for reaching its goals, but the goals themselves are quite valid. For example, George's Critic wanted him to be appreciated by his boss, to be successful, and to feel good about himself. There's nothing wrong with that.

When you genuinely connect with the Critic and it trusts you, it is much more likely to relax its need to judge you. It may actually listen when you tell it that the judgments are causing serious problems for the Criticized Child. The Critic is likely to be interested in better strategies for achieving its goals—and ones that don't harm your self-esteem. Recall our metaphor of the harsh parent and child. If you, as the third party, can show the parent that you sympathize with his situation and appreciate his efforts to parent his child well (even though he is actually harming the child), then he is likely to listen to you when you tell him that he needs to find a more helpful way of doing it.

In many cases, the Critic is a pariah in the internal system, hated by other parts because of the pain it causes. It often feels isolated and (ironically) judged by other parts. Or it may be involved in constant conflict with another part, such as the Inner Defender. So when you connect with the Critic, it often feels touched and relieved that its positive intent is finally recognized. And this helps to relieve some of the constant internal conflict you may have been suffering from.

Once you understand what your Critic has been trying to do for you, see if you appreciate it for trying to protect you and help you. Even if you don't like the pain that the Critic has been causing, perhaps you can see that its heart is in the right place.

This is a crucial shift for you. When you are open to the Critic in this way, you may see that it isn't just a powerful, nasty part after all. Your visual image of it may shift into something quite different. If it is hard for you to appreciate the Critic, you may still be blended with the Inner Defender. If so, go back to chapter 4 to work on unblending from the Defender.

When you feel appreciation for the Critic, communicate that directly to the Critic through words or through your heart. This is an important component of connecting with the Critic.

Once you have done so, check to see how the Critic is responding. Find out whether you have reached the Critic, whether it is taking in your appreciation, or whether it still doesn't trust you. Proceed with whatever additional work needs to be done to solidify your relationship with the Critic.

As the following transcript from George's session shows, often Critics will shift at this point, becoming less angry and judgmental, and more open to learning to work with you.

Jay: Do you have some appreciation for the Slave Driver's efforts on your behalf?

George: Yes, I actually do now. I see that it has really been trying to help me in this weird way.

J: OK. So let the Slave Driver know about your appreciation of it.

G: (laughs) It says, "It's about time that somebody saw me. You've been beating me up and trying to get rid of me for so long." Actually, I told the Slave Driver that I'm sorry. I didn't realize that it was trying to help me.

J: And how is it responding to you?

G: It's softening now. It's feeling relieved to not have to fight all those other parts in order to do its job. It says, "Somebody had to do this job. Somebody had to get you going, and no one else was doing it, so I had to. And then you hated me. And all these other parts tried to beat me up."

J: So it has been getting flak for doing the job it felt had to be done.

G: Yeah.

J: How is it responding to your appreciation?

G: It says, "This feels a lot better."

George's connection with the Slave Driver set the stage for further steps in healing. We will discuss these steps in the next chapters.

EXERCISE GETTING TO KNOW YOUR INNER CRITIC

Choose an Inner Critic part to work with. Using "Help Sheet 1: Getting to Know Your Inner Critic," do an IFS session in which you follow steps P1 through P5. Afterward, write down what you have learned about the part.

- What is it trying to accomplish by judging and pushing you?
- What is it afraid would happen if it didn't do this?
- What is it trying to protect you from?
- What is its response to you understanding and appreciating its efforts on your behalf?

Example

Here is how George answered these questions:

- What is it trying to accomplish by judging and pushing you? *Make me work hard and get my boss's approval.*
- What is it afraid would happen if it didn't do this? *I would be lazy and a complete failure. My boss would really think badly of me.*
- What is it trying to protect you from? *Failure and shame.*
- What is its response to you understanding and appreciating its efforts on your behalf? *Feels better, relieved, softening.*

HELP SHEET 1 GETTING TO KNOW THE INNER CRITIC

This is the first of three help sheets. This exercise, "Getting to Know the Inner Critic," will allow you to get used to using these help sheets, which is a crucial part of learning to work with IFS on your own. You can also refer back to the help sheets to review the steps of the IFS process.

P1 *Accessing the Critic*
If the Critic is not activated, imagine yourself in a situation in which it judges you. Get an image of it and hear what it says to you.

P2A *Unblending from the Critic*
Options for unblending:

- Remember that this is just an attack from the Critic, not the truth.
- Visualize the Critic as separate from you or choose an object to represent it.
- Find a part that is opposed to the Critic.

P2B *Unblending from the Criticized Child*
Check to see if you are feeling bad about yourself or believe that you are deficient. Options for unblending:

- Ask the Criticized Child to go into a safe place with a nurturing aspect of Self so you can help both it and the Critic.
- Step back into Self.
- Do a meditation to come into Self.

P3 *Unblending from the Inner Defender*
Check to see how you feel toward the Critic right now. If you feel compassionate, curious, and connected, then you are in Self; move on to P4. If you don't, then unblend from the Inner Defender as follows:

1. Ask if it would be willing to step aside (or relax) just for now so you can get to know the Critic part from an open place. Explain that doing this will help you to connect with the Critic and help it to change, and that you won't let the Critic take over and attack.
2. If the Defender is willing to step aside, check again to see how you feel toward the Critic, and repeat.
3. If it still won't step aside, ask what it is afraid would happen if it did, and reassure it about its fears.

P4 *Finding Out about the Critic*

Ask the Critic what it is trying to accomplish by judging you.

- Ask what it is afraid would happen if it didn't.
- Sense what exile it is trying to protect.

P5 *Developing a Trusting Relationship with the Critic*

You can foster trust by saying the following to the Critic (if true):

- I understand what you are trying to do.
- I appreciate your efforts on my behalf.

THE CRITIC CLUSTER

As you can see from what you have read so far, a whole cluster of parts arises in response to self-criticism. You have been learning about some of these parts and will continue to learn about more as you continue reading the book.

So far, you've worked with four of them, along with the Self:

- The **Inner Critic** attacks, judges, and dismisses you.
- The **Criticized Child** believes the attack and feels rejected, ashamed, and worthless.
- The **Protected Child** holds pain that the Critic is trying to keep you from feeling.
- The **Inner Defender** argues with the Critic, rebels against the Critic, or tries to banish the Critic.

Figure 1 depicts these parts and their relationships with each other. Notice that the Inner Defender is polarized with the Critic. This means they are at war with each other. The Self is able to cooperate with all the parts, even though they may be fighting each other. The Inner Critic is harming the Criticized Child, and the Inner Defender is trying to protect the Criticized Child. The Inner Critic is trying to protect the Protected Child.

Figure 1

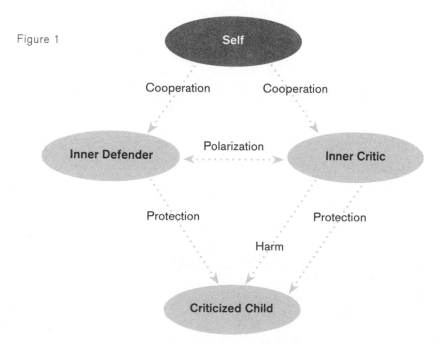

42

UNCOVERING THE ORIGINS
OF YOUR CRITICIZED CHILD

*Perhaps everything terrible is in its deepest being
something helpless that wants help from us.*

RAINER MARIA RILKE

et's look at common childhood situations that lead to the wounding of child parts and the activation of Inner Critic parts. You will use this information in this and the next chapter, when you learn to heal and reparent your Criticized Child.

JUDGMENT

Children are often judged by parents, family members, or other important people in their lives. If you were judged frequently or harshly, a child part of you that started out innocent and whole would end up feeling wrong, bad, inadequate, or worthless, depending on the kind of judgments you received. This is the part we call the *Criticized Child*. If the judgments were accompanied by anger, yelling, or physical abuse, the Child would also be traumatized.

Judgment can take a variety of forms. Almost all parents have certain standards for their children's behavior. Perhaps they expect their children to perform at a high level, not show emotions, be proper, or take care of others. If your parents loved and approved of you only when you met their standards, and they criticized you for failing to meet them, this would have an impact on your Criticized Child.

Perhaps your dad got frustrated with you because he had no tolerance for your process of learning, so he ended up criticizing you instead of helping you with homework. Maybe your mother didn't recognize that you were too young to know how to clean your room, so she flew off the handle at you. Your father may have tried to use criticism as a means of motivating you. He thought that judging you and comparing you to others would encourage you to work hard and succeed. Perhaps he focused only on your shortcomings and never praised you for your strengths or successes.

Any of these judgmental actions, if done repeatedly, would wound your Criticized Child and leave it with feelings of low self-esteem and incompetence.

The feeling of being inadequate can arise even if your parents didn't judge you. Suppose your mother was outgoing and you were introverted, or vice versa. Even if she didn't criticize you for being different, it would be natural for you, as a child, to feel that there was something wrong with you because you weren't like her. After all, she was your model for how a person is supposed to be. You might even try to be like her, but that would be impossible because your natural inclination is different. Your Criticized Child is likely to believe that there is something wrong with you for being different from her.

SHAME

Being shamed or ridiculed by your parents, teachers, or peers would cause your Criticized Child to carry shame or embarrassment. This experience could also prompt an Inner Critic to shame you in an attempt to keep you from doing again whatever led to your being shamed in the first place. Your Child might also carry shame if your parents or family felt ashamed about something such as poverty, their race or religion, or the way their community may have looked down on them. Children tend to take on the shame of their parents as their own, and it resides in the Criticized Child part.

PUNITIVE CONTROL

Children often do things that are dangerous to them, such as touching a hot stove or running into the street. Therefore, their parents need to stop them and teach them that these actions should be avoided. Maybe your parents over-reacted, screaming angrily at you if you so much as looked at the stove while it was on. Or when you darted toward the street, your parents not only grabbed your arm and scolded you, but spanked you and said that you were bad. If your parents overreacted this way, they may have accomplished their objectives, but your Criticized Child would be harmed in the process.

The same problem can happen when parents try to stop a child from hurting other children. If you hit other kids or took their toys for your own, as many children do, your parents needed to teach you not to do those things. However, if they yelled, "Stop that! You are bad!" this demeaning way of teaching would make your Child feel bad about having those natural impulses. This harshness would then activate an Inner Critic that wants to protect you from your parents. And the Critic (probably an Underminer or Guilt Tripper) is likely to use the very same harsh approach that your parents did. After all, they are the models for its behavior. So it will produce the very harm to your Criticized Child that it is trying to prevent.

REJECTION OR ABUSE

If your parents didn't want you, or if one of them abused you physically, your Criticized Child would end up feeling that it didn't have the right to exist or that it was dangerous to exist. So in order to keep you safe, a Destroyer Inner Critic may actually try to kill you or crush you so you aren't there, as strange as that sounds.

If a parent attacked you repeatedly, your Critic might blame you for the attacks, which would make your Criticized Child believe the attacks were your fault. The Critic does this so you won't fight back and be harmed even more. Taking on the blame also allows you to stay connected to the attacker, which is often crucial when you depend on a parent. It would be too scary to see how truly abusive your parent is. Your Critic would turn its anger on you since it isn't safe to get angry with your parent.

Another reason your Critic might attack you is to be in control of the attacks. This is preferable to being at the mercy of unexpected attacks from a parent. Your Critic would then feel as if it had some power in an impossible situation. Its attacks would also shut you down so you wouldn't be vulnerable when an attack came from your parent.

This feeling of being at fault can grow within you even without any blame or attack from outside. If something bad happened when you were a child—maybe you got very sick or one of your parents was depressed—your Criticized Child may assume it was your fault, even if there were no way it could have been. This assumption gives the Child the illusion of being able to change the situation: "If I did it, then maybe I can fix myself and stop it."

GUILT

Parents often use guilt to control children. Your parents may have told you that you were a bad person when you wanted special attention or demanded a particular Christmas present, which are perfectly normal behaviors for a child.

Perhaps they made you feel guilty by acting like martyrs and giving you responsibility for taking care of their pain and making them feel good. They may have blamed you for their problems and feelings, or even just turned to you for support too often. Any of these actions would make your Criticized Child feel guilty, and it might activate a Guilt Tripper Critic, which tried to stop you from doing the "bad" things or to force you to try to take care of your parents.

DIMINISHMENT

If you were judged or ridiculed whenever you were strong, visible, or capable, this would wound your Criticized Child. It would also trigger a Critic that tried to undermine you to keep you small, hidden, and safe. Your parents might have said, "Who do you think you are!" Perhaps you were rejected or abandoned for being powerful or standing out, or for being better than a sibling. Or maybe your parents felt bad about themselves when you outshined them in some way, and you felt responsible for their feelings. Any of these situations could trigger an Underminer Critic that tries to protect you by preventing you from being noticed.

MODELING VS. INTERNALIZATION

In most cases, our parents' means of controlling us will cause an Inner Critic part to start controlling us in similar ways. For example, if a parent used shame or guilt to get you to behave, your Critic will do the same.

The conventional psychological explanation says that your Inner Critic is simply a copy of your parent because you've *internalized* what your parent did. In this view, Critics don't have their own personhood and motivation. They simply mimic what your parent did. If this were true, the only solution would be to ignore your Critic, overpower it, or get rid of it.

However, IFS recognizes that Inner Critic parts aren't just mechanical copies of your parents. (This understanding is not unique to IFS. Voice Dialogue and other approaches that work with subpersonalities have come to the same conclusion.) Instead, Critic parts often *model* themselves after what your parent did when you were a child, but they have their own motivations in your current life. For example, if your father judged you as lazy, your Inner Critic might do the same thing, but not simply because it was copying your father. Most likely it would be judging you to get you to work hard so you wouldn't be judged by your father. Its *strategy* for protecting you is modeled after your father, but its *reason* for judging you is to protect you from your father.

You might say, "This doesn't make sense, because the Critic is causing a lot of damage right now." And you'd be right. It is making a misguided attempt to protect you from something that happened decades ago when you were young. The Critic doesn't realize the damage it is causing. The good news is that it *is* trying to help you, which means that you and the Critic are actually on the same team. So you can connect with it and work with it, which you couldn't do if your Critic were only a mechanical internalization of your father.

Some situations are more complicated. Suppose your father judged you as lazy to try to get you to work harder. Then, if your Inner Critic judges you as lazy to get you to work harder, it has modeled itself after both your father's motivation and his judgmental behavior. So the Critic looks even more as though it is simply a copy of your father. However, the central IFS view of parts still holds. The Critic is judging you because it thinks that doing so will help you, and therefore you can develop a cooperative relationship with it. That is the bottom line.

Keep in mind that any of these childhood situations can vary from mild to very intense. Some Criticized Child parts experienced judgments or other parental behaviors that weren't too harsh or only happened occasionally, and so they ended up with mild pain and feelings of inadequacy. Other child parts were seriously wounded and carry intense pain, crippling feelings of worthlessness, or perhaps even trauma. The intensity of an Inner Critic's attacks will often be proportional to the degree of wounding of the Criticized Child.

THE CRITICIZED CHILD AND THE PROTECTED CHILD

So far we have only discussed the Criticized Child, the wounded inner child part of you that is harmed and triggered by the attacks of the Inner Critic.

You will recall that the Inner Critic is a protector. It is judging you because it believes that doing so will keep an exile, a young child part of you that carries pain from the past, from being harmed or will protect you from that exile's pain. As explained in chapter 2, we call the exile the Critic is protecting the *Protected Child.*

In exploring the dynamics of the Inner Critic, we have come to realize that sometimes the Protected Child is the same exile as the Criticized Child and sometimes they are two different exiles.

For example, George's Critic, the Slave Driver, was trying to protect him from failing at work and being judged and disparaged by his boss. So it judged George in order to try to get him to work hard. George's Criticized Child felt inadequate as a result of these judgments. The Slave Driver was trying to protect an exile called the Little Boy, who was judged by George's father (as we will see later in this chapter). The Little Boy is actually the part that ends up feeling judged by the Slave Driver, so in this case, the Criticized Child and the Protected Child are the same—the Little Boy.

Jay's client Annie had an Inner Critic that was triggered whenever she wanted to speak up in her therapy group. It told her that she was stupid and useless and people would laugh at her if she tried to say anything. If she did speak, it would attack her afterward, telling her that what she had said was wrong and dumb. As a result, her Criticized Child part felt stupid and inadequate. This Inner Critic attacked her in an effort to prevent her from speaking and therefore being visible in the group. She had been abused as a child, and this Critic was afraid that if she made herself visible by speaking up, then she would get abused again. So Annie's Protected Child was an exile that was abused, while her Criticized Child was an exile that felt stupid. These are clearly two different parts, so in this case, the Criticized and Protected Children are different.

THE VALUE OF HEALING YOUR INNER CHILDREN

The wounds that the Criticized Child carries affect your feelings and behavior, even when your Critic isn't attacking. These wounds make you feel insecure, scared, worthless, ashamed, depressed, and so on. Therefore, healing your Criticized Child will help you feel better about yourself even before your Inner Critic changes.

It is especially helpful to work toward healing the Criticized Child when you're finding it difficult to work successfully with your Inner Critic. Often, if you heal the Child first, then the work with the Critic can proceed more easily. And the Inner Critic rarely tries to block you from working with the Child. Unlike other IFS protectors, the Inner Critic doesn't seem to mind allowing you access to the Criticized Child.

Your Inner Critic is also trying to protect your Protected Child or to protect you from the pain the Protected Child carries. So a good way to help your Critic to let go of its judgmental role is to heal the Protected Child first. Then the Critic doesn't need to protect it so much, so it is much more likely to be able to let go of its judgments and its attacking style. This is the normal IFS approach to working with protectors: you heal the exile they are protecting, and then you check to see if they can let go of their protective role.

In the next section, we will show how to heal either the Criticized Child or the Protected Child. The method for healing each of these exiles is exactly the same, so in the rest of this chapter, we will just refer to the Child, meaning either one.

GETTING PERMISSION TO WORK WITH YOUR CHILD

Before you work with an exile, you must get permission from any protectors that think working with it isn't safe; otherwise, they will sabotage the process. So you start by asking the Critic's permission to make contact with the Child. It usually gives permission fairly easily, but it is still important to ask. It also is a good idea to check to see if there are any other protectors that don't want you to access the Child, and then ask their permission as well. If a protector is reluctant to give permission, this is because it is afraid of what would happen if you worked with the Child. Ask it about this fear.

If the protector is afraid that you will be flooded by the pain of the Child, reassure it that you won't be diving in and becoming the Child. You will stay in Self and get to know the Child, so you shouldn't be flooded with pain. In some cases, you may first need to negotiate with the Child to not overwhelm you (see "Unblending from the Child" later in this chapter) before the Critic will give its permission.[1]

GETTING TO KNOW YOUR CHILD

The next step is to get to know your Child. First, you access the Child, and then, if necessary, you unblend from it.

Accessing the Child

You access the Child by feeling its emotions, sensing it in your body, or getting an image of it, just the way you would with any part. You might have an image of the Child as a wounded waif in a burned-out building. You might feel its pain as a knife in your chest or as a dark, empty hole in your gut. You might feel its hopelessness as a gray fog that seems never ending.

Unblending from the Child

Accessing the Child can bring up considerable pain. If necessary, unblend from the Child so you aren't flooded by its pain and so you can be available to comfort and help it.

You may have already done this unblending earlier in the IFS procedure (see chapter 3), but now that you are purposely accessing the Child to heal its pain, you may feel that pain more intensely—especially if you are working with a Child part that was seriously wounded. So you may need to repeat the unblending process.

You can unblend in a way that is similar to the procedure described in chapter 3: Ask the Child to separate from you so you can be there to help it. Make it clear to the Child that if it separates, you won't ignore it; you actually want to get to know it and heal it. Another approach is to step back from the Child, standing in a place where you aren't overwhelmed by its emotions.

UNBLENDING FROM THE CRITIC (AGAIN)

Now check to see how you are feeling toward the Child. If you are feeling curious and compassionate toward it, you are in Self and can get to know it. However, you might realize that you are feeling judgmental toward the Child, which means that you are blended with the Critic. Even though you unblended from your Inner Critic earlier in the process (see chapter 3), now that you are about to connect with the Child in a direct way, the Critic's judgments of the Child might be triggered, and it may blend with you again. You must unblend from the Critic, or from any other protector, so that you are fully in Self with respect to the Child. Only then can you heal it.

Critic parts sometimes feel that the Child is a bad part that has gotten you into trouble and caused pain in your life, so they naturally want to get rid of it. They don't want you to get to know it because that would bring up its shame and make you feel more inadequate or worthless. However, as you've learned, if you are dealing with the Criticized Child, the Critic is actually causing the Child to feel this way; the Critic usually doesn't understand this.

Explain to the Critic that if it lets you work with the Child, you can heal its pain and depression so it won't ruin your life anymore. Ask the Critic to step aside and let you get to know the Child and transform it. Once the Critic understands what you are aiming for, it will usually agree to this.[2]

GETTING TO KNOW THE CHILD AND CONNECTING WITH IT

The next step in healing the Child is to get to know it. You ask the Child to tell you about or show you the pain it feels in response to the Critic's attacks and the negative beliefs it has about itself. The Child often feels worthless, depressed, hopeless, hurt, or ashamed. It may believe that it is inadequate, bad, stupid, crazy, ugly, or repulsive.

You also need to develop a caring relationship with the Child. You will probably feel caring and compassion for the Child as you hear what it is feeling. Communicate your compassion directly to the Child, through words or through your heart. Then check to see how it is responding. Make sure it trusts you and is taking in your caring before going on.

If you don't feel caring toward the Child, you aren't in Self. Check to see what part has taken over and work with that part to get it to step aside, so you can relate to the Child from your heart.

ACCESSING AND WITNESSING THE ORIGINS OF YOUR CHILD

The feelings and beliefs that the Child carries may have two different causes. One is your Inner Critic's attacks, and the other is what happened in childhood—often criticisms from parents, teachers, or other children. The Child has been carrying pain that originated when you were young; the Critic is triggering this childhood pain and making it worse. In IFS, an important step in the healing process involves uncovering the situations that caused that pain in the first place.

Ask the Child to show you a memory or an image of what happened when you were young to cause it to feel so bad about itself. It will show you situations like those we discussed earlier in this chapter. Witness these early memories, relationships, and situations from Self, with caring and compassion for the pain of the Child.

Witness what the Child shows you about what happened and how it felt emotionally. It is usually not necessary for you to fully re-experience these feelings; it is enough just to witness them. However, your witnessing must be done from a place of empathy, not a removed or purely intellectual place.

Continue witnessing until the Child has showed you everything about these painful memories that it wants to. Then check to see if the Child feels that you understand how bad it was and, if necessary, have it show you more until it feels that you understand it.

GEORGE ACCESSES AND WITNESSES HIS CHILD

Jay writes: After my client George gained his Critic's trust, as described in chapter 5, he discovered that his Critic's positive intent was to protect him from being a failure and incurring his boss's disapproval. Our next step was to identify the exile that his Critic, the Slave Driver, was protecting and get the Slave Driver's permission to work with it.

> Jay: Ask the Slave Driver if it will give you permission to get to know that part it is protecting.
>
> George: It says, "Sure. Go ahead. I'm tired of doing this. Maybe you can do better."
>
> J: OK. Thank it for that.

As noted earlier, George's Criticized Child and Protected Child are one and the same.

> J: Now focus on the part that has been judged. Let me know when you have a sense of it.

G: (Pause.) OK. I can feel it in my belly. It feels empty and like a dull ache.

J: Can you see an image of what that part looks like?

G: (Pause.) Yeah. It looks like a little boy doubled over and holding his stomach. He looks really down.

Since George perceived his Child as a little boy, *the Little Boy* is the name he gave it.

J: How are you feeling toward him?

With this question, I was checking for two things: (1) If George was blended with the Little Boy. (2) If George was in Self with respect to the Boy.

If George were blended with the Little Boy, he wouldn't be able to answer the question because he would *be* the Little Boy. Since he was able to answer it, he probably wasn't blended with the Boy.

G: Well, mostly I feel interested in him. But there is a part of me that looks down on him. I don't want to have anything to do with him. He is such a loser, and he gets in my way so often these days, when I feel like I can't do things well.

J: So there is a part of you that is judging and dismissing him.

G: Yeah, I guess so.

Although George wasn't blended with the Boy, he wasn't in Self. He was blended with a concerned part, which might even be the Critic. So I helped him unblend.

J: OK. Explain to that part that if it lets us work with the Little Boy, we can heal him of his bad feelings about himself so he won't get in your way anymore.

G: That sounds hopeful.

J: See if that part would be willing to step aside so you can be open to the Little Boy, because that will allow us to do this healing work.

G: Yeah. It's willing.

J: Great. Check to see how you are feeling toward the Little Boy now.

G: I'm really interested in getting to know him.

Once George was in Self, we could move on to getting to know the Child.

J: OK. Ask him to tell you or show you what he is feeling.

G: He feels really bad about himself. He says he is a loser; he can't really do things well. He just thinks he can't pull it off, being successful. He's inadequate.

J: He believes he can't do things well.

G: Yeah. He'll never get seen and appreciated at work. (Pause.) He feels really sad about that. I can feel the sadness in my chest and eyes.

Now that we understood something about how the Little Boy feels, I wanted to discover the origins of these feelings in George's childhood.

J: Ask him to show you a memory or an image of what happened when he was little to make him feel this way.

G: I have a sense of my father being frustrated with him. Oh, he's trying to do homework, and my father is supposed to be helping him with it. But he's angry at the Boy.

J: How old is the Boy?

G: It seems like he's seven or eight. (Pause.) My father is totally frustrated with the Little Boy. He's yelling and screaming at him. He says the boy is stupid and lazy. "What's the matter with you, you lamebrain!"

J: Wow. Ask the Boy how that makes him feel.

G: Like a piece of crap. And scared, too. (Pause.) He feels really low, like there is something seriously wrong with him. Totally worthless.

J: And how are you feeling toward the Little Boy as you hear about this?

G: I feel a lot of compassion for him.

J: Let him know that. Communicate your compassion to him in some way.

Communicating his compassion would help George build his relationship with the Little Boy, which is important for healing in IFS.

G: He likes that. (Pause.) Now he feels angry, too. He's mad at his father for doing that. The Boy says, "It's not fair. I was doing my best. It was hard homework. And he didn't even give me a chance to learn it. He just flipped out."

J: Yeah. Let the Boy know that you welcome his anger. You are here to witness whatever he feels.

Anger is a valid feeling for an exile. It needs to be witnessed as much as more vulnerable feelings do.

G: OK. He is yelling at his father. (Pause.) Now the Boy is calming down.

J: See if there's more that he wants you to know about what happened or how it made him feel.

G: He felt all alone. There was no support for him anywhere. He just had to take this crap.

J: Yes, I understand that. (Pause.) Ask the Little Boy if that is everything, or if there is more that he wants you to know.

G: He felt ashamed of himself, like he wasn't worthy. A deep sense of wrongness. Like he was born flawed. This kind of thing, his father going bananas, happened many times.

J: Wow. That sounds awful. (Pause.) Ask him if he feels that you understand how bad this was for him.

Before George could move on to healing the Child, it was important that the Little Boy felt that the Self really understood its pain.

G: He says I get most of it, but he doesn't think I really understand how terrible he felt.

J: Ask him to show you whatever he needs to, so you really get that.

G: OK. Now I am feeling more of the Little Boy's shame and feelings of worthlessness.

J: Is it OK for you to be feeling that much of his pain or is it too much?

Here I was checking to make sure that George wasn't too blended with the Little Boy, because then the healing wouldn't be successful, and George might be retraumatized.

G: No, it's fine. I actually feel relieved to fully experience it.

Since George said he was OK with the pain, I knew he was still in Self, even though he was feeling some of the Little Boy's emotions. This is called *conscious blending*. You are aware that you are blended and can unblend easily if necessary.

J: Ask him if he now believes that you get how bad it was.

G: Yes, he does. He is happy to have someone understand how horrible it was. He feels lighter now.

With the witnessing complete, George and I were ready to move on to healing the Little Boy.

7

HEALING YOUR INNER CHILDREN

*There came a time when the risk to remain tight in a bud
was more painful than the risk it took to blossom.*

ANAÏS NIN

Now you're ready to heal your Inner Child (Criticized or Protected) of its wounds. This healing sets the stage for helping your Critic to let go of its judgmental role, which we will show you how to do in chapter 8. There are three IFS techniques for healing your Inner Child: *reparenting, retrieval,* and *unburdening.* They are done in this order, though any of them may not be needed in any given case.

REPARENTING YOUR CHILD

With reparenting, you (in Self) use your imagination to enter the scene of the childhood wounding and help the Child. You relate to the Child in the way it needed someone to relate to it back then. You give it what it needs to heal what happened or to change its experience. What it needs can be a variety of things, depending on what happened to produce the pain of the Child. If you are dealing with a Criticized Child, it will be one of the situations discussed in chapter 6. If you are dealing with a Protected Child, it could be anything.

Let's look at how to reparent a Child part that was judged, shamed, or attacked. There are two types of reparenting that this Child is likely to need.

1. **Protection.** You protect the Child from the criticism and attack by stopping the parent (or other person) from doing it. This can be done in a number of ways. You can imagine yourself standing between the parent and the Child in the original scene. You will be able to stop the parent because in Self, you can be bigger and more powerful than the parent, if necessary. Assert your strength and authority, and tell the parent that you won't allow them to criticize and attack the Child anymore. Explain to the parent that their criticism and attack are not helpful, and show them how this behavior is actually harming the Child. Most parents don't really want to hurt their children, so the parent figure may offer to change their behavior as a result of your intervention. You can also support the Criticized Child in standing up to the parent if it wants to do that.

2. **Validation and love.** Because you are in Self, you have the ability to give the Child the validation and love it needs. It may need you to accept it just the way it is. It may need your love and caring or your appreciation of who it is. Giving your Child your love, care, and acceptance will help the Child begin to feel good and valuable rather than bad and worthless.

Just telling the Child that it is OK or good isn't personal enough. The message needs to come from you in a personal way. Tell it, "I you love you and value you just the way you are." If your Child received conditional approval from its parents, tell it, "I think you're great just the way you are. You don't have to do anything at all to get my appreciation." This is crucial. The main message that your Child needs to hear is that it is lovable and valuable, that it is precious. However, it won't get the message just because you say it is these things (though saying them helps). It will get the message when it experiences that *you* love it and value it, that it is precious to *you*. This is a personal statement from you, not an abstract statement about the Child's worth. You will naturally feel this way toward it when you are in Self. If you aren't feeling this way, check to see if a protector is in the way, and work with that part to get it to step aside.

If your Child was blamed for something that it didn't do, tell it in no uncertain terms that what happened wasn't its fault. If your Child was criticized for not doing something that it shouldn't have been asked to do, such as taking care of an inept parent, let it know that the task wasn't its responsibility. If it was attacked for something that *was* its fault, help it see that it didn't deserve such nasty treatment.

Maybe it did need to learn to behave differently, but it isn't bad, and it didn't deserve to be attacked and shamed for its behavior. If the Child wants you to, you can even tell the parents that they shouldn't have treated it that way.

Even though it isn't possible to change what happened in the past, it is possible to change the way those experiences are held and structured in your psyche. In fact, brain research has shown that each time a memory is accessed, it is stored in the brain again. So by accessing these memories and then changing the experience, you are changing the memory to some extent. That is why reparenting is so effective.

RETRIEVING YOUR CHILD

Sometimes the Child will want to be taken out of the original harmful childhood situation and brought into a safe place. In your imagination, bring it into a place where it will be safe from judgment and shame and where it can be with you to receive your caring and appreciation. This can be a place in your current life, such as your backyard or your bedroom. It can be a place in your body, perhaps next to your heart. Or it can be any imaginary place that the Child would enjoy, such as a beautiful beach. The Child should be in charge of the retrieval, choosing whether or not it wants to be retrieved and where it would like to go.

UNBURDENING YOUR CHILD

A *burden* is a painful emotion or negative belief that an exile takes on as a result of what happened in childhood. A Criticized Child is likely to have taken on emotions such as shame, guilt, hurt, or depression. It might have taken on the belief that it is bad, inadequate, incompetent, worthless, unimportant, weak, mediocre, lazy, stupid, or ugly. If the Child was also attacked or harshly shamed, it may also have taken on the burden of feeling frightened and unsafe. A Protected Child could be carrying any type of pain. It is useful for the Child to release these burdens in an unburdening ritual done in your imagination.

First, check to see if the Child wants to release its burdens. It isn't always necessary, and the previous steps—witnessing, reparenting, and retrieval—may have done the healing that is needed. Then check to see if the Child is ready to let go of its burdens. If it isn't, find out what else needs to be done to prepare it to do so. Perhaps more witnessing is needed or a different kind of reparenting.

Once the Child is ready, have it locate where its burdens are lodged in or on its body. It can then choose how it wants to release them, so they will be carried away and transformed. Here are the options to offer: It can release them to light, have them washed away by water, or carried away by wind. It can put them into the earth, burn them up in fire, or do anything else that seems right.

After the burdens are released, the natural positive qualities and feelings of the Child will spontaneously arise. It is likely to feel valuable, lovable, and OK just as it is. It may also feel specific positive things about itself that were blocked by the judgments from childhood. It might feel good, strong, beautiful, competent, intelligent, or hardworking, for example. Help the Child to integrate these qualities by taking time to pay attention to what arises, feel it in its (your) body, and enjoy the experience.

HEALING GEORGE'S CRITICIZED/PROTECTED CHILD

Jay writes: After my client George had witnessed the pain of his Child, the Little Boy, and established a compassionate connection with him, we moved on to reparenting.

> Jay: Now I would like you to enter that scene with the Little Boy and your father, and be with the Boy in the way he needed someone to be with him then. Give him whatever he needs to feel better or to change what happened.
>
> George: (Pause.) Well, he wants me to hold him. (Pause.)
>
> J: Go ahead and do that.
>
> G: OK. And I'm telling him that he didn't deserve to be treated that way. That he was a good student; he just had some trouble with homework sometimes, and his father couldn't handle that.
>
> J: (Pause.) See if there is more that he needs from you.
>
> G: Yes. I'm telling him how much I appreciate the things he's really good at. Music and spelling and writing and sports—that he was smart and competent. (Pause.) But more importantly, I just appreciate him for being himself. I have a real sense of that now. I feel like I'm really in contact with him, and I just love him and value him. It's hard to explain.
>
> J: You don't need to. Just communicate that to him directly from your heart. That's more important than the words.
>
> G: Yes. He's taking that in.
>
> J: Good. (Pause.) See if there's anything else the Little Boy needs from you.
>
> G: No. He's feeling good. He's beginning to feel like he is OK as he is. (Pause.) He feels more at ease.

J: What does that feel like in his body?

G: He feels relaxed in his shoulders and a kind of bright feeling in his heart, like open and full.

The reparenting was complete. It doesn't seem like retrieval was needed, so I moved on to the unburdening step.

J: Great. Now ask him if he would like to release those burdens, those painful feelings and negative beliefs that he took on as a result of the way your father treated him.

G: Yes, he would love to do that.

J: OK. What are those feelings and beliefs?

G: Well, mainly feeling worthless and inadequate, and sad about that.

J: And where has he been carrying those burdens in his body or on his body?

G: In his heart, as a black weight, like a stone.

J: OK. We will help him to release it. He can give it up to light, or have it washed away by water, or blown away by wind, or put it into the earth, or burn it up in fire, or anything else that feels right.

G: He wants to bury that stone in the earth.

J: OK. Set up that situation for him.

G: We are going into a wilderness. (Pause.) I'm helping him take the stone out of his heart, and we're digging a hole on the side of a mountain.

J: Good. Take as much time as he needs. Feel that stone leaving his body as you do this.

G: The stone is in the ground. It's raining a lot, and the water is helping to dissolve the stone into the earth. And all the yuckiness is draining away and being renewed by the earth.

J: (Pause.) Let me know when it's all gone.

G: (Pause.) Yes, now it is.

J: Now notice what positive qualities or feelings are arising in the Boy now that this burden is gone.

With the burdens gone, the Boy could experience his natural, healthy state.

> G: It's similar to what happened a couple of minutes ago—a warm, good feeling in his heart. Like he is valuable, like he is precious, even.

> J: Wonderful. Take a few minutes to really enjoy that, to bask in it.

> G: (Pause, sigh.) It feels so good.

As you can see, healing the Child is beautiful work and very valuable in itself. And it also sets the stage for transforming the Critic.

EXERCISE HEALING YOUR CHILD

Do a session in which you heal a Criticized or Protected Child. Proceed through all the steps described in this chapter, using "Help Sheet 2: Healing Your Child" (page 64) as a guide.[1] Then take out your journal and fill in the information requested below.

- Child:
- If the Child was blended with you, how you unblended:
- If there were concerned parts, their fears and how you reassured them:
- The Child's feelings and beliefs:
- What situations caused it to feel that way:
- What happened in childhood:
- How that made the Child feel:
- What form(s) of reparenting you gave the Child:
- Burdens the Child carried:
- Where it carried the burdens in its body:
- What element the burdens were released to:
- Positive qualities that emerged:

Example

Here is how George filled out his sheet:

- Child: *A Little Boy doubled over and holding his stomach.*
- If the Child was blended with you, how you unblended: *N/A*
- If there were concerned parts, their fears and how you reassured them: *Part says he gets in my way by making me feel like I can't do things. I explained that we can heal him so he won't make me feel that way anymore.*

- Child's feelings and beliefs: *Feels really bad about himself, sad. He's a loser, inadequate. He'll never get appreciated at work.*
- What situations caused it to feel that way: *Work*
- What happened in childhood: *Father yelled at him and called him lazy and stupid.*
- How that made the Child feel: *Scared, worthless, all alone with no support. Angry with father.*
- What form of reparenting you gave the Child: *Held him. Told him he didn't deserve that treatment. Gave him appreciation and love.*
- Burdens the Child carried: *Worthlessness, inadequacy, sadness.*
- Where it carried the burdens in its body: *A black stone in his heart.*
- What element the burdens were released to: *Earth, water.*
- Positive qualities that emerged: *Warmth in heart, value, preciousness.*

HELP SHEET 2 HEALING YOUR CHILD

Use this help sheet for the exercise "Healing Your Child." You can also refer back to it as you review the steps of the IFS process later.

1 Getting Permission to Work with Your Child

If necessary, ask the Critic to show you your Child.
Ask its permission to get to know the Child.
If it won't give permission, ask what it is afraid would happen if you accessed the Child. Possibilities are:

- The Child carries too much pain. Explain that you will stay in Self and get to know the Child, not dive into its pain.
- There isn't any point in going into the pain. Explain that there is a point—you can heal the Child.
- The Critic will have no role and will therefore be eliminated. Explain that the Critic can choose a new role in your psyche.

2 Getting to Know Your Child

E1 *Accessing the Child*
Sense its emotions, feel it in your body, or get an image of it.

E2 *Unblending From Your Child*
If you are blended with the Child:

- Ask the Child to contain its feelings so you can be there for it.
- Consciously separate from the Child and return to Self.
- Get an image of the Child at a distance from you.
- Do a centering/grounding meditation.

If the Child won't contain its feelings:

- Ask it what it is afraid would happen if it did.
- Explain that you really want to witness its feelings and story, but you need to be separate to do that.

Conscious blending: If you can tolerate it, allow yourself to feel some of the Child's pain.

E3 *Unblending Concerned Parts*
Check to see how you feel toward the Child.

If you aren't in Self or don't feel compassion, unblend from any concerned parts. They are usually afraid of your becoming overwhelmed by the Child's pain or the Child taking over.

Explain that you will stay in Self and not let the Child take over.

E4 *Finding Out about Your Child*

- What do you feel?
- What makes you feel so bad about yourself?

E5 *Developing a Trusting Relationship with Your Child*

- Let the Child know that you want to hear its story.
- Communicate to it that you feel compassion and caring toward it.
- Check to see if the Child can sense you, and notice if it is taking in your compassion.

3 Accessing and Witnessing Childhood Origins

- Ask the Child to show you an image or a memory of when it learned to feel this way in childhood.
- Ask the Child how this made it feel.
- Check to make sure the Child has shown you everything it wants you to witness.
- After witnessing, check to see if the Child believes that you understand how bad it was.

4 Reparenting Your Child

- Bring yourself (as Self) into the childhood situation and ask the Child what it needs from you to heal it or to change what happened.
- Protect it from being attacked or shamed.
- Communicate to it your love, acceptance, and appreciation for it.
- Check to see how the Child is responding to the reparenting.
- If it can't sense you or isn't taking in your caring, ask why and work with that.

5 Retrieving Your Child

One of the things the Child may need is to be taken out of the childhood situation. You can bring it into some place in your present life, your body, or an imaginary place.

6 Unburdening Your Child

- Name the burdens (extreme feelings or beliefs) that the Child is carrying.
- Ask the Child if it wants to release the burdens and if it is ready to do so.
- If it doesn't want to, ask what it is afraid would happen if it let go of them. Then handle those fears.
- How does the Child carry the burdens in or on its body?
- What would the Child like to release the burdens to? (light, water, wind, earth, fire, or anything else)
- Once the burdens are gone, notice what positive qualities or feelings arise in the Child.

7 Releasing the Critic

- See if the Critic is aware of the transformation of the Child. If not, introduce the transformed Child to the Critic.
- See if the Critic now realizes that its judgmental role is no longer necessary.
- The Critic can choose a new role in your psyche.

8

TRANSFORMING YOUR INNER CRITIC

I'm not afraid of storms, for I'm learning to sail my ship.

LOUISA MAY ALCOTT

After you have gotten to know the Inner Critic and formed a trusting relationship with it, as described in chapter 5, you are ready to transform it. This chapter shows three ways to help an Inner Critic release its judgmental role:

- Showing the Critic the healed Child and seeing if the Critic no longer needs to protect it.
- Showing the Critic how much it is harming the Child and seeing if it wants to stop doing so.
- Negotiating with the Critic to allow you (in Self) to handle a situation that the Critic is concerned about.

RELEASING THE CRITIC AFTER HEALING THE CHILD

If you have been following the process outlined in this book, you have now done some significant healing with the Child that the Critic was protecting.

Now that the Child is feeling good about itself, the Critic is likely to be able to stop judging you. In most cases, the Critic has been judging you in a misguided attempt to prevent you from acting in ways that would lead to your being judged, attacked, or shamed by your parents. It didn't realize that you are now an adult and no longer under its power. Now that the Child is feeling good about itself, it isn't likely to be so hurt by any new judgments, so the Critic can relax. Furthermore, if someone in the present does judge you and the Child gets hurt, you can now take care of the Child just as you did in the reparenting step of the last chapter. So for all these reasons, the Critic no longer needs to try to protect the Child.

Check with the Critic to see if it is aware of the work you have just done with the Child and how the Child has been healed. If the Critic isn't aware of this, introduce the Critic to the healed Child so it can see what has changed in it. You want the Critic to be able to see that the Child is feeling OK now and can't be hurt very much by judgments.

Once the Critic recognizes the change in the Child, ask the Critic if it still feels a need to perform its protective role of judging you or if it can now let go. Often it will be ready to let go, and it may even be happy to give up such an onerous job. You may need to discuss any fears it has about letting go and explain how you will handle any judgments that come up in the future.

If your Critic isn't ready to let go of its role, ask what it is concerned would happen if it did. Its answer will give you important information about additional work that may need to be done. Perhaps there are other exiles the Critic is protecting, and it can't let go until they are healed, too. Maybe the Child is only partially healed, and more work must be done with it. Perhaps the Critic doesn't trust that the Child is truly healed, and it needs more time to experience the shift. Other ways to help the Critic feel safe enough to relax and let go are presented later in this chapter.

Once the Critic has let go of its judgmental job, it can choose any other job in your psyche that it wants. It might want to be a supporter for the Child, which means it would become your Inner Champion (see chapter 10). It might choose a healthier version of the job it has been doing, which would make it your Inner Mentor (see chapter 11). Or it could choose an entirely different role or just decide to take a vacation. When one of Bonnie's clients gets to this stage, she offers the Critic the option of joining a wisdom council, a heart collective, or a grounding team comprised of parts in the person's psyche.

GEORGE'S STORY, CONTINUED

Jay writes: When George finished healing his Criticized/Protected Child, the Little Boy, we turned our attention back to his Inner Critic, the Slave Driver. I asked George to check if the Slave Driver was aware of the healing work George had done with the Little Boy.

George: Yes. It has been paying attention the whole time. It's kind of amazed that this has happened.

J: Ask the Slave Driver if it might now be willing to let go of judging you.

G: (Pause.) Well, it feels somewhat better, but it is still concerned that I won't work hard enough to be successful.

J: Ask the Slave Driver what it is afraid would happen if you didn't work that hard.

G: It is afraid of not getting approval from my boss.

J: Remind the Slave Driver that the Little Boy is feeling fine about himself, so maybe the Slave Driver doesn't need to try so hard to get approval from your boss.

G: It's considering that. (Pause.) Well, it doesn't feel a desperate need for approval anymore, so I can sense that it is relaxing and doesn't have so much charge around this whole thing.

J: Good.

G: But the Slave Driver still isn't ready to completely give up judging. It is afraid of my being lazy and getting bad performance reviews.

The Slave Driver has relaxed some, but more is needed for it to fully transform. George needs to negotiate with the Slave Driver to let him handle his work from Self. Later in the chapter, we'll see how this happens.

EXERCISE RELEASING THE CRITIC AFTER HEALING THE CHILD

Choose a Child part that you have healed using the steps in the last chapter. Re-access that part and confirm that it is still in the healed state. If it is, follow the steps described above to help your Inner Critic release its judgmental role, if it is ready to.

Then in your journal, answer the following questions:

- How does the healed Child feel?
- What are the Critic's concerns about letting go?
- How did you reassure it?
- What is the new role it would like to have in your psyche?

Example

Let's look at how George answered the questions about the healed Child and his Critic.

- How does the transformed Child feel? *Warm and good about himself.*
- What are the Critic's concerns about letting go? *Worried that I won't work hard and will get judged by my boss.*
- How did you reassure it? *Explained that I will work well and my boss isn't unreasonable.*
- What is the new role it would like to have in your psyche? *For now it just wants to relax.*

INTRODUCING THE CRITICIZED CHILD TO THE CRITIC

In the previous section, we discussed introducing the Child to the Critic so the Critic could see how the child has been healed. However, there is a different use of this introduction that can be a powerful approach to change, even before the Child has been healed.

Let's assume that you have gotten to know the Critic and have formed a trusting relationship with it, as described in chapter 5, but you haven't yet healed the Child. Perhaps you had a traumatic childhood, so healing the Child will take awhile. Maybe you have an important situation coming up in which your Critic is likely to be activated, and you don't have time to go through the healing process with the Child before it happens. Here is a quicker way to release the Critic.

As you've learned, many Inner Critic parts are paradoxically causing the very pain that they are trying to prevent. In fact, often they are causing far more pain than what they are protecting against. They are stuck in the past, when there was real danger or harm, and they are doing their best to prevent it now. But the only way they know how to do this is to criticize, and they have no clue about the pain this criticism is causing. We can change the situation by making them aware of the impact of their criticism.

First access the Criticized Child and get to know it, as described in chapter 6. You especially want to get clear on how the Child has been hurt by the Inner Critic's attacks and how it is continuing to be hurt by the Critic. Then introduce the Child to the Inner Critic, so the Critic becomes aware of how it has been harming the Child. Ask the Critic if it was aware of the pain it was causing the Child.

Your Critic might say something like, "Oh my gosh. I didn't know I was causing pain. That's not what I intended. I was just trying to help you not be judged by people." Ask the Critic how it feels now that it knows what has really been happening. It may say that it is sorry to be hurting the Child.

In some cases, the Critic is not only causing the Child pain, but it is also producing the very behavior in the Child that it is trying to prevent. For example, an Inner Controller Critic might be trying to prevent the Child from overeating by judging it. However, its judgments will make the Child feel ashamed and depressed, which may cause it to turn to food to dull the pain. You can ask the Critic to notice that it is causing this behavior in the Child. This information will give it even more motivation to stop its attacks. Now ask the Critic if it might be willing to relax and decrease its judgments. It will often agree.

If it isn't ready to shift, ask the Critic what it is afraid would happen if it let go of judging. It may still feel that its protection is necessary. When you find out what it is afraid of, reassure it about these concerns. If the Critic is willing, see if it wants to choose another role in your psyche. Perhaps it would be willing to modulate its statements to a more benign form.

Introducing the Child to the Critic is useful either before or after the Child has been healed (or partially healed). Sometimes the Inner Critic can't let go of its judgmental role very easily, even after the Child has been healed. In this case, showing the wounded Child to the Critic can facilitate this process.

But this introduction doesn't work with all Critics. Some already know that they are harming the Child. For example, some Critics hurt the Child purposely to undermine your self-confidence so you won't take risks that they think are dangerous. For these Critics, this introduction won't be effective.

EXERCISE INTRODUCING THE CRITICIZED CHILD TO THE CRITIC

Choose a Critic that you already have a trusting relationship with. Access the Criticized Child that is being harmed by it, as described above. Then answer the following questions in your journal:

- What is your image of the Child?
- What are the Child's feelings and beliefs?
- How is Child being harmed by Critic?
- Introduce the Critic to the Child. Did the Critic know it was harming the Child?
- How did the Critic respond to learning that it has been causing the Child pain?
- Is the Critic now ready to let go of criticizing?
- If not, what is it concerned about?
- If so, what new role is the Critic willing to take on, or how can it change its statements from harmful to helpful?

Example

- What is your image of the Child? *A five-year-old hiding his face in a corner.*
- What are the Child's feelings and beliefs? *He is not interesting or valuable because he is not intellectual.*
- How is the Child being harmed by Critic? *Critic tells him no one cares about him because he is dumb.*
- Introduce the Critic to the Child and find out if the Critic knew it was harming the Child. *No.*
- How did the Critic respond to learning that it has been causing the Child pain? *Surprise and chagrin.*
- Is the Critic now ready to let go of criticizing? *Maybe.*
- If not, what is it concerned about? *Critic wants me to be more intellectual so I can make intelligent conversation and be liked.*

NEGOTIATING FOR SELF-LEADERSHIP

Here is another approach to releasing the Critic that doesn't depend on healing the Child first. Now that you are beginning to connect with your Critic, it may be willing to cooperate with you and learn a different way to respond when a situation triggers it. When a situation arises that activates your Critic, such as writing a paper, going out on a date, or interviewing for a job, it usually starts pushing and attacking you. You can learn to negotiate with it so that it will allow *you* to take the lead in these situations.

Your Inner Critic became extreme in childhood because it was dealing with a dangerous or harmful situation—for example, being ridiculed when you tried to get attention or always being told that your work wasn't good enough. And it believes that the same harm is going to happen now in your current adult life. Furthermore, when you were little, there wasn't a mature Self there to help, so the Critic had to handle this painful state of affairs all on its own. Now that you are an adult, you have a competent, perceptive Self to help in difficult circumstances. Even if you haven't had very much access to your Self in the past, it is now starting to become available because you are reading this book, doing this IFS work, and learning to access it.

However, your Critic doesn't realize that your Self is now available to help, so you need to make this clear. Explain to your Critic that because you are in Self, you can handle this situation and make good decisions. Tell the Critic that it doesn't have to use its judgmental strategy to protect you because you don't need as much protection, and you have a better way of handling difficult situations. Since your Self and your Critic are now connected, the Critic is more likely to listen to you and trust what you say.

In childhood, you were attacked, rejected, or shamed for some reason. Now, from the place of Self, you can explain to the Critic that the current situation is very different from what happened then. You are no longer vulnerable and dependent like a child. You are autonomous and are no longer under the power of your parents. You have many strengths and capacities as an adult (possibly because of previous work you have done on yourself) that you didn't have as a child. For example, you are more grounded and centered. You may be more assertive, more perceptive about interpersonal situations, better able to support yourself financially, and so on. You have already accomplished things in your life and overcome various obstacles. You are an adult with much greater ability to handle yourself. You have friends, maybe a spouse or lover, perhaps a community you belong to, a support group, or professionals you can rely on. You have people you can turn to, if necessary.

This means that you aren't in danger the way you were as a child, and your mature Self is available, which wasn't possible when you were young. Therefore, your Critic can relax and allow you to handle things. You can explain to the Critic how you will handle any situations that come up now that it might be worried about. Ask it to trust you and allow you to be in charge of these circumstances.

If your Critic relaxes, there may be certain healthy capacities that it could bring to these situations, and you could help it do that. If this is so, explain to your Critic how it can help in a healthy way.

Example: Negotiating for Self-Leadership with the Perfectionist

The Perfectionist Inner Critic demands that your work be perfect and attacks you when it thinks it isn't. Sometimes a Perfectionist will keep you from writing, performing, or producing anything, even if no one will see your efforts. This Critic especially tends to be activated when you are learning a skill or when you are experimenting in a creative way with something new. The Perfectionist is afraid to let you come up with or produce anything because the result may not be very good at first, and that is frightening for this part. You were harshly criticized or shamed in the past, and the Perfectionist is trying to prevent this from happening again. This Critic is the cause of writer's block for many people.

How might you negotiate with this type of Perfectionist Critic? There are two possibilities:

- If no one will see what you produce, you can explain to the Perfectionist that you are safe from criticism. Initially, you will be producing work that may not be very good, but that is to be expected, and it may even be necessary for your learning or experimentation. Your work is just a rough draft and will be improved or even rewritten many times as you go. Therefore, you don't have to worry about its quality at all. You won't show your work to anyone until you have improved it, and therefore you will be safe.

- If you will be showing your work to a teacher, a colleague, or someone else, you can explain to the Perfectionist that these people know that your work is at an early stage or that you are just learning or experimenting. They don't expect you to be excellent yet. If they do criticize your work, they are only aiming to help you learn or improve what you are doing. Therefore, the Perfectionist can relax and allow you to operate without being concerned about your output. Remind the Critic that these people aren't your parents or grade-school teachers (or whoever originally criticized you).

- Even if someone who looks at your work *is* harsh, and you end up being judged or even shamed for what you produce, you can handle that. You are resilient and self-supporting; you won't fall apart. You have much more internal strength for dealing with this situation than you did as a child. You have friends and colleagues to turn to now.

Your Perfectionist *does* have an important role to play in helping you to improve your work, but its input must come at the right time, which is after you have produced something that is far enough along for evaluation to be useful. Then the Perfectionist, like a good coach, can offer constructive feedback and suggestions for improvement. If you are writing, it shouldn't comment after each sentence, but instead at the end, when you have finished what you are producing. Then its input will be helpful.

If you are in the early stages of a project, or if you are just learning a skill or are experimenting with something new, the Perfectionist's critique probably isn't called for yet. It will be needed later on, when your work is somewhat polished. By holding off until then, the Perfectionist won't get in the way of your learning or creativity. And by working this way, your Perfectionist will become an Inner Mentor (see chapter 11).

Ask your Perfectionist if it would be willing to take the chance to let you produce work without criticism and see what happens. Ask it to let you (in Self) be in charge, and reassure it that there isn't much danger and that you can handle whatever may happen. You are asking it to allow you to take the lead. You will then let it know the right time for it to bring in its critical skills in a helpful way. It is more likely to agree to this if you have already connected with it and it trusts you.

This is one example of how negotiating for Self-leadership can be done. You can adapt this technique to whatever type of Critic you have and the kinds of situations that trigger it.

Negotiating for Self-leadership can be useful either before or after the Criticized Child has been healed. It provides additional reassurance for the Critic, which will likely make it feel more comfortable letting go of its judgmental role.

NEGOTIATING WITH GEORGE'S CRITIC

Jay writes: My client George illustrates another way of successfully negotiating with a Critic for Self-leadership.

> George: But the Slave Driver still isn't ready to completely give up judging. He is afraid of my being lazy and getting bad reviews from my boss.

> Jay: Let me check on something. Have you actually been working adequately on the project at your job? Consider this question from Self, not from the Slave Driver's perspective.

I wanted to find out whether the Slave Driver's fear of George not working well is valid or an outmoded childhood fear, so I checked with George in Self to see what the reality was.

> G: For the most part, I have been working well. Occasionally I procrastinate. Usually that's because I'm afraid that I won't do a job well enough, when there's a feeling of inadequacy.

J: Is it the Little Boy who feels inadequate?

G: Hmm. That's an interesting question. (Pause.) Yes. It is that part. That's what throws me off. And then a procrastinating part comes in to try to avoid feeling inadequate by not trying at all.

J: So explain to the Slave Driver that this isn't so likely to happen now that the Boy is feeling good about himself.

Since the Little Boy was healed, there wasn't the same need for protection from the Slave Driver. My suggestion was aimed at helping the Slave Driver realize that.

G: The Slave Driver is listening and seems to be relaxing some.

J: And if the Slave Driver stops judging you, the Little Boy can continue to feel confident. In fact, explain to the Slave Driver that its judgments have been part of the problem.

Showing the Slave Driver how its judgments had been hurting the Little Boy is similar to introducing the Critic to the Child so the Critic could see the harm it had been causing.

G: It's really thinking about that. It is shocked to even consider that. (Pause.) Well, it's trusting me a lot more now, so it's willing to consider that it should stop judging me. But it's still worried about my not working hard enough.

J: Explain to it that you agree with its goal of working hard in order to do a good job. Remind it that you have been working well most of the time, and that, as an adult, you have good work capacities.

Since the Slave Driver still had concerns, we needed to address them, one at a time. We explained that George had the capacity to work well when in Self.

G: I'm telling it that I can plan my work, pace myself, keep up my motivation, and ask for help when I need it. And I commit myself to working well, so it doesn't need to push me. (Pause.) It likes that idea, but it's still worried about getting judged by my boss.

J: OK. Remind the Slave Driver that you aren't a child anymore, and you're no longer under your father's power.

G: I also told it that my boss is pretty reasonable most of the time, unlike my father.

J: Good. You could also explain to the Slave Driver that if your boss does judge you and it hurts the Little Boy, you will take care of the Boy just like you did earlier in the session, so he will end up feeling good about himself.

G: I'm also telling the Slave Driver that if my boss does get unreasonable, I will talk to him about how he is treating me. I won't just put up with it. (Pause.) That makes the Slave Driver feel better. It says it's willing to try this approach and see if it works.

J: Great! Thank it for that.

We had finally addressed the Slave Driver's worries enough that it was willing to experiment with allowing the Self to lead.

EXERCISE NEGOTIATING FOR SELF-LEADERSHIP

Choose a Critic that you already understand and have a good relationship with. As you work through each step or when you are finished, write down the following information in your journal.

- Your image of Critic:
- What it says to you:
- What situations trigger it:
- What it is trying to protect you from:
- Childhood fears of Critic:
- Why those fears aren't valid now:
- What resources you bring to the situation now:
- How you will handle the situation effectively:
- What the Critic can offer the situation in a healthy way:

Example

Let's look at how George filled out the answers for this exercise.

- Your image of the Critic: *The Slave Driver*
- What it is trying to protect you from: *Being judged by my boss.*
- Childhood fears of Critic: *My father being angry with him about doing homework.*
- Why those fears aren't valid now: *I'm no longer a child under my father's power. My boss is more reasonable than my father was.*

- What resources you bring to the situation now: *The capacity and commitment to work well.*
- How you will handle the situation effectively: *I will work well, and if the boss does judge me, I will take care of the Child's feelings.*
- What the Critic can offer the situation in a healthy way: *Not there yet, but willing to let me lead.*

HELP SHEET 3 TRANSFORMING YOUR CRITIC

You can refer to this help sheet while you are working on the steps in this chapter and when reviewing all the steps of the IFS Inner Critic process.

Introducing the Criticized Child to the Inner Critic

- Access the Criticized Child.
- Understand its pain, especially how it gets hurt by the Critic.
- Introduce the Child to the Critic.
- Ask the Critic if it realized it was hurting the Child.
- Ask the Critic if it is ready to let go of its judgmental role.
- If necessary, reassure it about any concerns it has about letting go.
- Invite the Critic to choose a new role.

Negotiating for Self-Leadership

- Describe to the Critic what your capacities are as an adult in Self.
- Explain to the Critic why the current life situations it is concerned about are not as dangerous as when you were young.
- Tell it what you intend to do in these situations to handle them safely.
- Ask the Critic to relax and let you lead in these situations.
- If appropriate, explain to the Critic how it can aid you in a healthy way.

TRANSFORMING AN INNER CRITIC
WITH A LEGACY BURDEN

The finest inheritance you can give to a child is to allow
it to make its own way, completely on its own feet.

ISADORA DUNCAN

So far in this book you have learned that Inner Critic parts are actually
trying to do something positive for you, even as they cause pain and
hardship. However, there is another aspect to many Inner Critics. They
are often modeled after a parent or other significant person from childhood. For
example, Sarah's Critic, the Attacker, from chapter 4, modeled its behavior after
the attacks that were rampant in her family when she was a child. It was trying
to protect an exile, and its methods were learned from her parents.

Many therapy approaches see Inner Critics only as internalized versions of
our parents, without recognizing their protective nature. IFS recognizes both
aspects of Inner Critics.

Sometimes it isn't enough to discover a Critic's positive intent and heal the
exile it is protecting. In order to help your Critic to fully let go of its attacks, you
may also have to deal with how the Critic learned to attack.

THE LEGACY BURDEN

In IFS, the protective role that a Critic has adopted is called its *burden*. When a Critic is playing a role (carrying a burden) that it modeled after a parent, this role is called a *legacy burden*. If your father pushed you to work very hard and criticized you when you didn't, you may develop an Inner Critic that does the same thing. It has taken on this legacy from your father. If your mother always compared you negatively to your sister or friends, you may develop a Critic that does the same thing.

Critics may acquire legacy burdens in ways other than directly modeling themselves after a parent. A part can acquire a legacy burden by taking on some aspect of a parent or of an entire line of ancestors that you didn't have direct experience of or even know about. However, with Inner Critics, you usually do have direct experience of the parent's behavior.

Often a Critic models its *style* of criticism on a parent's style, even though the Critic may criticize you about different issues. For example, Joan's mother criticized her for being sloppy and judged her for not keeping herself as neat, clean, and organized as her mother wanted. She did this by calling Joan names—*slob, lazy girl.* Joan had long ago disavowed her mother's extreme focus on neatness, so her Inner Critic didn't judge her about that. But Joan did have a Critic that judged her for not being attractive enough to men. And guess what? That Critic attacked Joan by calling her names, except that now the names are related to the attractiveness issue—*loser, ugly girl,* and so on. Same style, different content.

A legacy burden might not only come from a parent, but also from an entire ancestral line. Maybe your father pushed and judged you about not working hard enough, and maybe his father did the same to him, and perhaps his father's father and the entire line of male ancestors were burdened by this extreme need to overwork. Each of these men probably had different life circumstances and motivations for their overworking, but the essential pattern is similar. An ancestral burden like this can have a profound effect on you without your being aware of it.

DISCOVERING A LEGACY BURDEN

How do you know if one of your Inner Critics got its style of criticism from one of your parents? Let's suppose you have followed the process laid out in this book so far. You have gotten to know one of your Critics and discovered what exile it is protecting. You have healed that exile and the Critic is now less intense with its attacks, but it is still attacking you. For the Critic to fully relax, you may have to help it let go of its legacy burden as well.

It can be helpful to reflect on whether or not your parent (or some significant person in your childhood) had the same style of criticism as your Critic, but to find out for sure what is going on, ask the Critic. For example, you might say, "Show me where in childhood you learned to put me down as a strategy for getting me to work harder. Where did you get the idea that judging me would accomplish this end?" The part is likely to show you a scene in which your parent was putting you down.

There are two reasons for asking the Critic to show you its history. One is for you to find out if the Critic has a legacy burden. The other is to help the Critic to realize that it has a legacy burden and where that burden came from. In fact, the latter is the more important reason. Often the Critic just thinks that criticizing is the way anyone would go about trying to help you. However, once it sees that it learned this from your father, for example, the Critic may now be more open to realizing that there are other, more effective, ways to achieve its goal. You can also help the Critic to see that these other ways are likely to be less hurtful.

TRANSFORMING AN INNER CRITIC LEGACY BURDEN

To let go of an Inner Critic legacy burden, first you must develop a trusting relationship with the Critic, which includes assuring it that you agree with its goals for you. If it is trying to get you to work hard, for example, so you will be successful, make sure it realizes that you want to work hard and be successful too. Just let it know that you don't think its strategy of judging and attacking you is working and that you want to develop a more effective strategy for achieving this goal.

Once it is clear that the Critic has a legacy burden, ask the Critic if it would like to let go of this burden and perhaps learn a more effective way of helping you. We have found that Critics with legacy burdens are surprisingly amenable to such requests. They are much less attached to protecting their exiles than other protectors. If it says yes, there are three ways to release the burden.

The first way is to do an unburdening ritual just like you would with a Child, as described in chapter 7. In this case, the burden is the Critic's judgmental role and style of attacking. You discover how the Critic is carrying this burden in or on its body and then release the burden to a healing presence (e.g., light, water, wind, earth, or fire).

Your second option is to pass the burden back to the "parent" it came from, have them add their own burden to it, and then pass this combined burden back to a healing presence. If the legacy burden involves an entire ancestral line, then have each ancestor add their own burden and pass it back down the line, through generations known and unknown, and then finally release it to the healing presence.

After the burdens have been released, ask the Critic what positive feelings or qualities (such as love, strength, or relaxation) are arising, and then pass these back to the parent and perhaps all through the ancestral line to take the place of the burdens they have released. This way, all ancestors are unburdened and transformed, not just your part. (This method was developed by Michi Rose, a former IFS trainer.)

Finally, you can work with the "parent" to help them let go of their critical role and other burdens and come into the present. This method was developed by Bonnie and will be described next in detail, followed by two example sessions that she did with clients who were dealing with Inner Critics with legacy burdens.

At this point, you may be wondering what is actually going on with all these methods. You are working with an internal image/entity in your psyche that looks like your parent. Maybe this is simply your internal representation of the parent, and you are imagining unburdening them. So by unburdening the parent part, you are undoing the legacy burden that came from that part.

On the other hand, maybe you're doing more than that. Maybe you are actually working with the spirit of your parent in some way and helping them to heal. Maybe the image of your parent isn't just your internal representation of the parent but is something that goes beyond the boundaries of your psyche. This perspective is consistent with other experiences that have been described in IFS work that seem to go beyond the individual psyche. We don't presume to know the answer to this question. All we know is that these methods of unburdening your "parent" work.

UNBURDENING THE PARENT

This method can be used when the image of the Inner Critic that spontaneously arises looks like one of your parents. You will feel like you are actually dealing with the parent rather than simply a part of you. You work with this internal entity as if it were your actual parent to help it let go of its burdens, which releases the Inner Critic from its attacking role.

There are potentially six steps to this process:

1. **Getting to Know the Parent.** Recognize the parent and say hello. Explain that you (in Self) are the adult version of the child he or she raised. If necessary, show the parent how old you are and what has transpired in your life, so he or she realizes your current stage of maturity and the capacities you have now that you didn't have as a child.[1]

2. **Retrieving the Parent into the Present.** Ask the parent if they would like to come out of the past and into the present to get help. They are almost always happy to do this.

3. **Witnessing the Parent's History.** Ask the parent to show you what happened in their childhood or adult life that led them to become judgmental toward you and others. The burden usually involves the parent believing that they must be a certain way (successful, self-effacing, perfect, for example); that you, as their child, also had to be that way; and that the best approach to make someone be that way was to judge them. The parent's history often involves being judged in this same way by their parent, your grandparent, along with many other important incidents and relationships. (Don't worry about whether or not the information you receive in this way is completely accurate. Most of the time it will be, but more importantly, it reflects the often unconscious way your psyche holds this situation.)

   Open your heart in compassion for your parent's pain, and communicate your caring to them. Make sure they have showed you everything that is important.

4. **Reparenting the Parent.** In some cases, it may be appropriate to have the grandparent (or another ancestor) reparent the parent. A transformed grandparent becomes the good parent that the parent needed as a child, treating the parent in the loving supportive way that they needed but didn't get back then. This reparenting allows the parent to behave in a more loving and appropriate way toward you and shifts the legacy to one of acceptance and love.

5. **Unburdening the Parent.** Ask the parent if they would like to give up their burden. If the parent says yes, then help them engage in an unburdening ritual. This can be either the normal IFS unburdening ritual (see chapter 7) or the legacy unburdening involving their entire ancestral line as discussed earlier in this chapter, as the second option under "Transforming an Inner Critic with a Legacy Burden." When this ritual is complete, the parent (and maybe all the ancestors) will be healed of their burdens, and your Inner Critic part will have let go of its strategy of attacking you.

6. **Transferring Positive Qualities.** After the burdens have been released, ask the parent what positive feelings or qualities (such as love, strength, or relaxation) are arising or what qualities they would like to have to help them in the future. Then pass these qualities back through the ancestral line so all the ancestors can have them.

Another option is to become aware of the positive qualities you received from the parent. These are often quite accessible because the burden has been released and, along with it, your anger toward the parent. Take some time to feel these qualities and celebrate your connection with the parent.

In the case where there is an ancestral line involved, a third option is to go back through the ancestral line until you discover an ancestor who was healthy and had something to offer with respect to inner criticism. Have them pass those healthy qualities forward to all their descendants, including you and possibly your children and future generations.

TRANSFORMING JIM'S LEGACY TASKMASTER

Bonnie writes: Jim was a successful corporate executive. His easy, affable manner belied the internal tension that drove him toward success. He was the corporate man, the good guy, everybody's buddy, but relentlessly self-critical on the inside. He had trouble taking time off, chronically worked late, and never felt he had done enough. His internal tension was beginning to manifest in physical ailments. His gastroenterologist suggested he seek psychotherapy because of the pressure he kept putting on himself.

Jim came from a military family, where he was the youngest of six brothers. Genetically gifted athletes, everyone in the family was very competitive. They always excelled in school sports, skied together, and roughhoused constantly. The military moving around solidified the "band of brothers" mentality. Though also a competent athlete, Jim was naturally more sensitive than the rest. He had more artistic inclinations, which he identified as being like his mother's.

His father, Arthur, was an iconic figure in the family. Jim looked up to him and sought his approval. This wasn't easy to get, and Jim felt disappointed that he couldn't please his father very much.

Being the youngest son by a number of years, Jim wasn't allowed to join his brothers on certain family adventures, leaving him feeling left out, small, and inadequate. When he *was* included, his father wasn't able to adjust his expectations to his youngest son's age. Jim was pushed to keep up with his brothers and ridiculed when he couldn't.

Jim developed an Inner Critic that constantly judged him for not working hard enough, not achieving enough, not being enough. Its aggressive expectations caused him to push himself unmercifully and to feel inadequate at a deep level, despite his outward successes.

In his IFS therapy work, Jim accessed this Inner Critic and discovered that it had the voice and face of his father. I had Jim work with this father part as if it were actually his father, Arthur. As he did, Arthur opened up to Jim about his own relationship with *his* father, Jim's grandfather, a successful self-made, Depression-era businessman. It turned out that Arthur, too, had felt that his father was never satisfied with him. Arthur also had a softer, more aesthetic side that was totally unacceptable to *his* dad. Arthur's decision to join the military got him out of the house at an early age and was aimed at snuffing out his gentler leanings.

This line of men were all carrying a burden of "being a tough man," which was reinforced with harsh judgments. It came as a legacy burden from Jim's grandfather through his father to Jim. Jim's drive toward success was actually more Arthur's drive than his own.

In working with this legacy burden, I encouraged Jim to openly dialogue with Arthur about Arthur's life and struggles. We took this work back one more generation and invited in Edward, Arthur's father. I encouraged Arthur and Edward to have a dialogue, with Jim playing the voices of each of his ancestors. Arthur was able to tell his father that he didn't want to be pushed to be a success. Edward was able to hear this and see Arthur more realistically. He reparented Arthur in the way Arthur wished he had treated him as a child. In turn, Arthur let Jim know that he actually identified with Jim more than his other sons and was therefore harder on him. He let Jim know how proud he was of him.

Jim was able to listen to Arthur's sadness and remorse about the way he had treated Jim, and Jim offered him forgiveness and healing. Together, the two of them released their burden of ignoring the softer side of themselves and pushing themselves to be successful at all costs. They also offered this healing to Arthur's father and the men of even earlier generations in this family.

Once these burdens were gone, Jim and Arthur were able to access their natural gentleness, aesthetic appreciation, and feelings of positive self-worth. Jim was able to take in Arthur's genuine pride in him.

This process completely shifted Jim's Inner Critic. It no longer judged him and pushed him. As Jim gradually integrated this experience into his life, his Inner Critic allowed him to be easier on himself about work. He began to leave the office at a more reasonable time, take vacations, and focus on creating balance in his life. He not only had a much more relaxing, enjoyable life, but he also felt much better about himself and therefore more confident in his dealings with people.

TRANSFORMING MELANIE'S LEGACY GUILT TRIPPER

Bonnie writes: Melanie had just become a grandmother. She was excited when her son, Scott, had a little boy. He was ecstatic and ready to be the best possible parent. She wanted desperately to be supportive, but nagging inside her was a terribly uncomfortable feeling about difficulties in her relationship with Scott when he was a child.

Though she loved Scott very much, there had always been some distance between them. She knew that some of this tension was a result of times when she had been harsh and impatient with Scott. In these situations, she would be acting as usual, dealing with the normal ups and downs of raising Scott and his two sisters, and then she would suddenly fly into a rage at him with very little provocation.

Melanie felt awful about these incidents. She had explored them in different ways, but the bottom line was that she couldn't explain these outbursts and, more importantly, couldn't forgive herself for them. She felt internally flawed, guilty, and damaged.

Now, with the birth of her grandson, her self-hatred about her past was coming to the surface, so she sought psychotherapy with me. As we began to listen to her parts, a brutal Guilt Tripper Critic emerged, saying it would never forgive her for what she had done. It appeared in the form of her father, in the same cold, angry, and menacing demeanor that she remembered from him.

In other therapy she had fought with this Critic. She had tried to stand up to it, control it or banish it. Nothing had worked. I helped her to clear away her negative reactions to this Critic and become openly curious about it. In response, the Critic actually softened and was willing to engage with her.

I had Melanie interact with this Critic as if it were her father, because that was the way she perceived it. Melanie had a difficult relationship with her father. He had wanted a son and had been demanding and cruel to her.

When she engaged with this Father Critic from an open place, he actually softened and began to talk to her. When she asked, he told her some of the details of his difficult history. He, too, had been at the mercy of a rejecting parent. He had left home at an early age to get away from his father and joined the armed services. He had some difficult war experiences that left him feeling that he would never again trust anyone in authority.

Melanie's heart melted as she heard his story. I encouraged her to invite him to leave the past and come into the present of her life. He readily agreed. Her softness towards him brought up an image of her father cuddling into her neck and licking her face like a cat.

She forgave him for the way he had treated her, and the father allowed Melanie to help him release his burden of guilt about his past actions. Her father's father was also carrying the burden of being harsh and rejecting and feeling guilty about that. And in fact, many of her ancestors also carried such burdens.

We invited the father to help release these burdens of pain and guilt all through the ancestral line. At first he was resistant to this idea, but he eventually allowed us to help the previous generations let go of their past, too.

By healing the father and his ancestors, she was actually helping her own Guilt Tripper Critic to release its twin burdens of guilt and of making her feel guilty. As a result, Melanie felt forgiven for what she had done to her son, and a sweet feeling of compassion arose in her heart toward herself. Melanie's relationship with her son and her grandson is now characterized by openness and softness. She told Scott about her therapy work, and he was hopeful that this family legacy will stop in his mother's generation.

EXERCISE RELEASING THE LEGACY BURDEN OF AN INNER CRITIC

Access an Inner Critic part, get to know it, and develop a trusting relationship with it. If its image is not that of one of your parents, then ask where it learned its strategy for judging you. If it identifies a parent as the source, go through the steps of the second unburdening method described above. Enter the information about what happened in your journal:

- What was the parent's burden?
- Did this burden go back through an entire ancestral line?
- What happened when the Inner Critic passed its burden back to the parent (or ancestors)?
- What was the burden released to?
- What positive qualities arose in the Critic now that its burden is gone?

If the Critic does look like one of your parents, use Bonnie's approach to unburdening it. Enter the information here about what happened:

- What is the parent's name?
- How did you show the parent that you are a competent adult?
- Was the parent interested in coming into the present?
- What was the parent's history around inner criticism?
- If the grandparent reparented the parent, how was this done?
- If the parent did an unburdening ritual, how was this done?
- What positive qualities arose in the parent?

10

AWAKENING YOUR INNER CHAMPION

The only service a friend can really render is to keep your courage by holding up to you a mirror in which you can see a noble image of yourself.

GEORGE BERNARD SHAW

The Inner Champion is an aspect of the Self that supports us and helps us to feel better about ourselves. It encourages us to be who we truly are rather than fitting into the box our Inner Critic creates for us. It is a magic bullet for dealing with the negative impacts of your Inner Critic. One way to think about your Inner Champion is to see it as the ideal supportive parent that you always wished you had. It is an aspect of the Self that responds in a helpful way to Inner Critic messages. It helps you to see the positive truth about yourself instead of the negative lies from the Inner Critic.

This chapter will help you get in touch with your Champion, so you can evoke it when you need it in the face of an Inner Critic attack. If it feels frightening to you to evoke an Inner Champion, feel free to skip this chapter. There are other ways to free yourself from your Inner Critic.

THE BIRTH OF THE INNER CHAMPION

Bonnie writes: In 2006, as I was planning the first Women's Inner Critic Workshop, I had a difficult professional moment. I made a thoughtless comment that I believed had serious consequences for a client. As it turned out, my actions were not the cause of her difficulties, but there were a few weeks when I was being extremely hard on myself. I was on an airplane to New York, planning the workshop and trying to quiet my own Inner Critic, a demonic Guilt Tripper.

The methods I had used in the past—confronting it, separating from it, or justifying myself to it—were not working. It felt as if I needed bigger guns—more power and capacity. I had an image of a personal guide who loved me and supported me. This guide, which was clearly an aspect of me, had the capacity to stand up to my Inner Critic, which gave me some emotional space so I could think and regain my center. The guide had the perspective to see the entirety of who I am, not just a moment of lapse. It was able to comfort and nurture the child part of me who was taking the brunt of the criticism. And it had the practical ability to develop a clear action plan to make sure my client was OK.

That was how the idea of the Inner Champion was born. The Inner Champion can be developed and cultivated to be a vibrant resource in your psyche. It nurtures and cares for you, provides a wider vista of guidance, and helps you take charge of your inner life and actions.

HOW THE INNER CHAMPION HELPS US

Jay's client George learned to activate his Inner Champion when his Slave Driver Critic was judging him and pushing him to work harder. His Champion said to him:

- You can trust yourself to do a good job at work.
- I accept you just the way you are.
- You can accomplish what is needed, in a stress-free way.
- You have the right to a relaxed work life.
- You can be a very successful and valued employee without killing yourself.
- You have the right to work reasonable hours so you can enjoy the rest of your life.

Hearing these statements helped George to feel confident and relaxed at work and to have time for his family and leisure activities.

Our Inner Champions can help us in four different ways: setting boundaries for your Critic, nurturing you, providing guidance, and action planning.

Let's look at each, with examples of statements the Champion can make with each approach.

Setting Boundaries with the Critic

Your Inner Champion can set limits on your Inner Critic to get you some emotional space in which to feel into yourself and take stock. It can make statements to your Inner Critic such as the following:

- Your judgments aren't helpful.
- Now is not a good time for this.
- Your judgments are making things more difficult.
- Please step aside right now; your attitude is causing problems.
- I know you want to protect, but your approach isn't working.
- I know your heart is in the right place. Let me show you a more effective way to accomplish your goals.

Nurturing You

Your Inner Champion can make supportive, nurturing statements to you that help you to accept and appreciate yourself. For example:

- I completely accept you no matter what.
- I love you.
- I care about you.
- You have accomplished many valuable things in your life.
- I appreciate your qualities and capacities.
- You have a lot to offer people and the world.
- You are special to me.
- I value you just for being you.
- You are beautiful and whole just the way you are.
- You already are everything you need to be right now.

Providing Guidance

Your Inner Champion can make encouraging statements to help guide you on your way and support you to move ahead in your life.

- You can trust yourself.
- Your struggles just represent where you are now in your growth.
- You can do it.
- I support you in whatever you take on.

- You are doing well. You are on your way.
- I want you to have your heart's desire in life.
- I'm proud of you.
- You will find a way forward.
- You will discover what it is you are meant to do.
- You have the right to be yourself and do things your way.

Action Planning

Your Inner Champion can make suggestions to help you plan actions you need to take.

- You have the right to take your time and do things at your own pace.
- Congratulations on accomplishing that step.
- You can overcome whatever obstacles are in your path.
- You can find supportive people in your life.
- You can correct course whenever necessary; doing so doesn't mean you have failed.

A HEALTHY VERSION OF THE INNER DEFENDER

In chapter 4, we introduced the Inner Defender, the part of you that argues with your Inner Critic and tries to convince it that you really are a good person. It may fight with the Critic over its judgments of you—for example, "You're wrong. I *am* adequate. Look at all the things I have accomplished in my life." This part is attempting to counter the Inner Critic in an adversarial way. However, its efforts create inner conflict because the Critic will fight back, which often just reinforces its negative messages.

The Inner Champion is the healthy version of the Inner Defender. It doesn't fight with the Inner Critic, though it may set some limits on the Critic in a mature way. The main thing it does is support you (and your Criticized Child) in the face of the Critic's attacks. It helps you to feel self-confident not by fighting with the Critic but by supporting and encouraging you. This way doesn't promote inner discord.

SEVEN FLAVORS OF INNER CHAMPIONS

Since our Inner Champion helps us deal with our Inner Critic, there is a specific version of the Inner Champion for each of the seven types of Critics.

In the face of a **Perfectionist** Critic, your Inner Champion supports your right to *not* be perfect. It reminds you that it is only human to make mistakes and that making an error doesn't mean there is anything wrong with you. It reminds you that you are totally OK even if you don't get everything right. It supports your right to have balance in your life—to rest, take care of yourself, and enjoy life. It knows that many jobs just need to be done well enough, not to super-high standards. It has the wisdom to know that sometimes it is important to go with the flow and let things evolve rather than trying to get everything perfect right away. It supports you in being a learner who doesn't have to know everything to start with. It knows the meaning of "rough draft."

An **Underminer** Critic tries to make you feel inadequate so you won't take risks that it considers dangerous. In response, your Inner Champion can discern when there is real danger and when there isn't. It understands that you have many more resources, both inner and outer, available to you than when you were a child. It knows that you have inner strength and resilience and that you have people to help and support you. So it realizes that you can handle most difficulties that arise from taking risks or being powerful. Furthermore, it can recognize when you are in a situation that *isn't* dangerous, in which you are unlikely to be attacked for being large and visible. Therefore, it knows that you can venture out and succeed. It holds a vision of you being powerful and innovative and making your mark on the world.

If you have a **Taskmaster** Critic, your Inner Champion has a two-pronged attitude: it helps you work hard and accomplish things, and it also recognizes that you are just fine the way you are. Although this may sound paradoxical, this kind of self-acceptance actually supports you in developing yourself. Your Champion also recognizes your strengths and special qualities, which helps to build your self-confidence. It encourages you to succeed in a relaxed, easygoing way. It doesn't expect you to overwork or to be relentless in achieving your goals. Yet it knows that you can achieve what you set out to do.

An **Inner Controller** Critic judges you harshly to try to stop you from over-eating, using drugs, or indulging in other dangerous substances or activities. In response, your Champion tells you that your real needs and desires are OK and that you are fine just as you are. It supports you in being relaxed and trusting your decisions about what you eat or what you do. It also supports you in being centered and in touch with your body, which naturally brings moderation. It supports your capacity for healthy pleasure and sensuality in life, which is satisfying enough that there is no need for overindulgence.

With a **Guilt Tripper** Critic, your Inner Champion supports you in feeling good about yourself in the face of guilt about your past actions. When you examine your true values, if you feel that what you did wasn't wrong, like leaving home or marrying someone you love who is of a different race or religion, the Inner Champion supports you in not feeling guilty about it. It tells you that you were acting in integrity and that you are a good person. It tells the Guilt Tripper to back off because its outmoded values came from your family or culture and don't reflect your truth.

A **Molder** Critic tries to get you to be a certain way based on the values of your parents or culture. In response, your Inner Champion helps you to see that the Molder's values are not the only good way to live your life. It supports you in determining your own choices of lifestyle and way of being. It tells you that you are a good person even if you choose to live your life in a way that goes against your upbringing and culture. Your Champion supports you in being yourself and living according to your deepest values. It wants you to actualize your true nature and live according to your highest calling, whether or not this calling fits any external idea of what is right.

In the face of a **Destroyer** Critic, your Inner Champion affirms that you have the right to exist. It confirms that existence is your birthright. Your Inner Champion loves you and cares for you. It has great compassion for your suffering and wants you to feel good and whole. It holds you close and tells you that you are precious. This Champion nurtures you in the most fundamental bodily way, not only because you need it, but also because it loves to be close to you.

Sometimes the Destroyer Critic turns anger or aggression inward; it turns anger toward you that was originally meant for other people in the outside world. Your Inner Champion can redirect that anger toward where it belongs. It affirms that you have the right to be angry with people who have hurt you or neglected you. It also tells you that you have the right to set limits, to protect yourself, or to be powerful—and yes, these may involve ending a job or relationship that isn't right for you.

These descriptions are intended to inspire you and offer possibilities, not to limit or define your experience. Feel free to allow your Champion, this helpful aspect, of yourself to emerge in whatever way is unique to you.

It may seem from these descriptions that your Inner Champion is being too easy on you and isn't helping you to look at issues of yours that need to be worked on. This is because prompting self-exploration is the job of your Inner Mentor, which we will explore in the next chapter.

EXERCISE AWAKENING YOUR INNER CHAMPION

Your Inner Champion is a natural part of your Self—who you really are. You can often get in touch with your Champion just by tuning in to that place in you that supports you in being yourself and feeling good about yourself. However, it can also be based on supportive or inspiring people, such as those from your past or current life, well-known people that you don't know personally but admire, or even noble figures from literature or the arts.

To access your Inner Champions, first find a quiet place to sit and relax. You might play some gentle, evocative music.

Ground yourself by breathing deeply in your belly, feeling your feet on the floor, your back on the chair, your shoulders relaxed, your jaw slightly open.

You are going to take a trip back in time. Look for moments when you felt seen, appreciated, acknowledged. You could start from early childhood and work your way up to the present or go backward from the present time. Let the memories of these moments come as they will—images, sensations, smells, feelings.

Remember a specific time when you were recognized, encouraged, or supported by someone. A wise person may have stood up for you, guided you, or just let you know that they saw your pain. This person may have been a teacher, coach, neighbor, friend, parent, or friend's parent.

Think of a past moment in your life when someone championed you, when someone really saw you and heard you, someone recognized you and had faith in you. What did this person say to you? You can base your Champion's words on their words.

You can also base your Champion's wisdom on people you admire because they lived their lives with integrity. Think of people who were kind and supportive to others, or people who held far-reaching visions for themselves and those they loved. You may be drawn to a famous person, such as Mahatma Gandhi, Margaret Mead, Nelson Mandela, Oprah Winfrey, Amelia Earhart, Winston Churchill, Rachel Carson, Barack Obama, Gloria Steinem, Paul Newman, Katharine Hepburn, Georgia O'Keeffe, or Michael Jordan.

You can also look for figures from books, TV, or the movies—characters you admired for their ability to champion others, such as the trainer who had faith in *Rocky*, the spirited trio in the movie *Nine to Five*, the father in *Father Knows Best*, Gandalf the wise wizard from the *Lord of the Rings* trilogy. Or you may find strong images from mythology—Athena, Mercury, Artemis. As you find figures to inspire your Inner Champion, ask them to step over to your side, to be on your team, to surround you with their strength. They will help you in dealing with your Inner Critics and moving forward in your life.

BRIGITTE'S STORY

The following story illustrates the power of using your Inner Champion to resolve Inner Critic issues—in this case, a Molder Inner Critic.

Brigitte moved around a great deal as a child. Her British father and Californian mother started out in the United States, tried to live in London, and then, after their divorce, ferried her back and forth. She was a shy child, and not having siblings made the experience of adjusting to a variety of cultures all the more difficult. As an adult, she lived in Saudi Arabia with her husband and then moved to New England.

Early on she was aware of an internal voice that said, "Just fit in." She was often teased or rejected by schoolmates for her accent, eating different foods, thinking differently, or just not being "in the know." She tried to adapt, learn, and change to be accepted. She dreaded the playground; it was a minefield of possibilities for being humiliated.

In her adult life she was plagued by an obsession to "do the right thing." Because each culture she lived in was so restrictive in terms of social expectations and mores, she had to repeatedly retool her behavior. She was always struggling with anxiety about being accepted and becoming part of the social order. Once, as an adult, she dressed in casual Californian garb to go to a church committee meeting. Then her Molder Critic really got down on her. It was very frightened that she would be rejected by the people at the church.

Her husband had no sympathy for her struggles. He thought she was making too big a deal out of them. He could let things roll off his back and didn't understand her painful shyness and how the simplest social slight was agonizing.

In her IFS work, Brigitte was able to appreciate how her Molder Critic had tried to help her learn and relearn what was "right." The Molder was trying to protect a little girl part inside her who had suffered a lot of trauma in being repeatedly rejected. She got permission from her Molder to access this exile and expressed deep compassion for her.

The concept of an Inner Champion was delightful to Brigitte. Her vivid imagination evoked a goddess of a Champion in a gauzy blue costume, complete with magic wand. She appeared "just like magic!" Brigitte said. This Champion enfolded the suffering Child in her immense wings and told her that she was lovable just the way she was. She made the Child feel accepted and safe when she was in pain. This Goddess Champion also stayed with Brigitte step by step in her social encounters, encouraging her to be herself. Whenever her Molder Critic started to berate her for not trying to fit in, her Champion would come in and support her in being herself.

Things began to change for Brigitte fairly quickly. With her Champion by her side, she was more courageous in her social encounters. Her quick wit and sense of humor stood out, and she felt seen and accepted. She reported being happy for the first time in her life: "Happiness just arises, and it is me."

EXERCISE INNER CHAMPION STATEMENTS

In this exercise, you will be invoking your Inner Champion to support you in the face of specific Critic attacks. You will be crafting statements in your journal that you want your Inner Champion to say to you. These might be statements that you already hear from inside or ones that you are beginning to hear more often. Or they can simply be statements that you would like to hear from an Inner Champion, even if you never have.

Remember that your Inner Champion always supports you. It doesn't tell you what to do or not do. It tells you what you *can* do or what you have *the right* to do. It doesn't say, "Don't give up"; it says, "You can succeed if you stay with it." It doesn't say, "Take it easy"; it says, "You have the right to take it easy." It makes personal statements directly to you. Rather than saying, "You are lovable," it says, "I love you."

- Write down a situation in which your Inner Critic gets activated and attacks you:
- Think about what you would like to hear from your Inner Champion in this situation. What do you want it to say to you?
- When is this situation likely to happen over the next week or two?
- If your Inner Critic gets activated, evoke the image (or images) of your Inner Champion from the previous exercise. Imagine this figure saying the above Inner Champion statements to you. How does that make you feel?

Example

Here is what one person wrote for this exercise.

- Write down a situation in which your Inner Critic gets activated and attacks you: *Giving a talk at work.*
- Think about what you would like to hear from your Inner Champion in this situation. What do you want it to say to you? *You can do it. I appreciate your creative ideas. People will be interested in what you have to say. They want you to succeed because that means they will learn something. I care for you and support you no matter what happens.*
- When is this situation likely to happen over the next week or two? *Project report on Wednesday.*
- If your Inner Critic gets activated, evoke the image (or images) of your Inner Champion from the previous exercise. Imagine this figure saying the above Inner Champion statements to you. How does that make you feel? *Calmer and more confident.*

11

CULTIVATING YOUR INNER MENTOR

I am not discouraged, because every wrong attempt
discarded is another step forward.

THOMAS ALVA EDISON

Our Inner Critics are trying to perform a function that is necessary in our psyches. We all need the ability to look at ourselves realistically to see how we could change and improve. We want to be aware of the ways we act that don't align with our values. We need to be able to see when we are hurting someone unnecessarily or when we aren't working to our potential. We must recognize when we are doing something dangerous or compromising to our health, or when we are being shortsighted because of a need for immediate gratification. The problem is that the Inner Critic performs this function in a way that undermines our self-esteem and self-confidence. Sometimes it criticizes us in ways that are simply false and totally unnecessary.

However, there are times when there is a grain of truth in the judgments of our Critic and even times when a judgment contains wisdom we have been ignoring. In these cases, the problem isn't the content of the Critic's judgment, but rather the harsh, nasty, condemning way the judgment is delivered. The message doesn't have to be expressed this way; there is another option.

It is possible to have a gentler and wiser voice inside—a voice we call the *Inner Mentor*. This part is a healthy version of the Critic. It performs this necessary function in our psyches in a positive way, whereas the Critic does it in a destructive way.

YOUR INNER MENTOR

Suppose you are a parent and your child doesn't clean up his room the way you asked him to. If you act like an Inner Critic, you might say in a harsh, loud voice, "What a mess! You're so dumb. Can't you do anything right?" However, if you instead act like an Inner Mentor, you might say in a kind, supportive voice, "Honey, that's not quite what I was looking for. Let me show you how to clean up a room. Let's do it together."

Recall Jill from chapter 1, who was nervous before a date and binged on cake. Her Critic screamed at her, "You look fat! No man will ever marry you." Suppose that instead of her Critic saying those things, her Inner Mentor had said, "OK, that wasn't the best response to the nervousness you were feeling. It would be better to stay with your feelings than to overeat, but I know that is hard. I will help you forgive yourself and find a better way next time." Then Jill wouldn't have spent the next twenty-four hours worrying about her date. She could have been confident and excited and had a good time over dinner.

This is how your Inner Mentor can treat you—with love and acceptance. It can also help you clearly see when the way you acted wasn't aligned with who you want to be, and it will help you take action to remedy the situation.

GEORGE'S INNER MENTOR

When the Inner Critic transforms, it often becomes the Inner Mentor because the Mentor is a healthy version of the Critic. When George's Slave Driver Critic transformed, it became a kind coach.

George's Inner Mentor said, "Most of the time you work quite well, but every once in a while you procrastinate on a project, and it gets you in trouble. You don't need to work harder, you just need to notice when you are avoiding a task so you can get back on track. I will help you do that. It seems to happen when you're feeling insecure about a job you have to do. Then you start playing games on your computer and reading the news too much. When that happens, I will signal you so you realize what is happening. Then I'll help you face the job you have been avoiding. This will not only get you better reviews from your boss, but it will also make your life easier because you won't be forced to pull an all-nighter every once in a while. I will also help you use IFS to work on that Procrastinator part and the insecure exile it is protecting. I will remind you of this at your next session."

These words helped George to overcome his problem with procrastination without undermining his self-confidence in any way.

YOUR INNER MENTOR AND INNER CHAMPION: PARTNERS IN SUPPORT

You need both your Inner Mentor and your Inner Champion in order to feel good about yourself and function well. They naturally and easily work together. Your Inner Champion supports you in feeling good about yourself and moving ahead in your life. Your Inner Mentor helps you to see where you can improve yourself.

For example, suppose you lost it and yelled at your daughter, making her upset. A Guilt Tripper Inner Critic might castigate you, saying, "You are a horrible parent. How could you do that terrible thing to her? And you've done it so many times before. You don't deserve to have such a wonderful child. You are ruining her life. You should be shot!" Your Inner Champion might say, "I know you're really a good mother. Everyone gets angry occasionally. You really love her and want the best for her. Pick up the pieces and move on from here." This is the support you need, especially in the face of an attack from your Guilt Tripper.

However, this isn't all you need. You also need a constructive voice to help you look at what went wrong and what you can do about it. Your Inner Mentor might say, "I know that's not the way you want to treat your daughter, because you love her. Let's see what you can do to keep this from happening again. Your life has been very stressful lately, and you need to take better care of yourself. You could notice when you are starting to get angry with her and remember not to take it out on her. You could explore what's behind your anger, which may have nothing to do with her. You could take a brief timeout when you find yourself starting to lose control." Your Inner Mentor would say this in a kindly, helpful manner, without judgment.

You can see that the Inner Champion and Inner Mentor are a great pair. They each supply something important. They each support a key healthy capacity in you. The Inner Champion supports your capacity for self-esteem, and the Inner Mentor supports your capacity for self-improvement. The Inner Champion is a healthy version of the Inner Defender. The Inner Mentor is a healthy version of the Inner Critic.

In some situations, the Inner Mentor is not needed. Sometimes your Inner Critic judges you about something that is just plain false; there is no grain of truth in its accusation. For example, the Critic says you are worthless and will never amount to anything. Then you only need your Inner Champion to support your self-esteem. There is no need for you to change anything.

In IFS terms, the Inner Champion and Inner Mentor can be seen as aspects of Self or as parts in their natural, healthy state. They manifest healthy qualities that intrinsically exist in you unless they are blocked, usually by the Inner Critic. In this sense, they are aspects of Self. However, when the Inner Critic transforms and chooses a new job in your psyche, it often chooses to become the Inner Mentor, since that is the healthy version of the Critic. And the Inner Defender can transform into the Inner Champion. In these cases, the Mentor and Champion would be seen as healthy parts. In our view, all healthy parts can be seen as more delineated, personified aspects of Self, so there is no need to choose between these two perspectives. We see the Champion and Mentor as both healthy parts *and* as aspects of Self.

SEVEN TYPES OF INNER MENTORS

We have delineated a specific version of the Inner Mentor for each of the seven types of Inner Critics. Each Mentor embodies a certain wisdom for dealing with these seven issues in your life. Again, these descriptions are intended to inspire you with possibilities, not to limit or define your experience. Feel free to allow these helpful aspects of yourself to emerge in whatever way is unique to you.

If you have been procrastinating or not working enough to get what you want in life, your **Taskmaster** Inner Mentor will help you, in a kindly, supportive way, to see that something needs to change. It will aid you in devising a work plan that can be successful. It will encourage you to work on the parts in you that are avoiding tasks that need to be done. It also recognizes that goals change over time, and it is flexible in what it expects from you while still gently encouraging you to do more.

Your **Perfectionist** Inner Mentor can differentiate between a situation in which your current efforts are enough for your purposes and one in which you really do need to improve. If you have a part that tends to be too loose or turn in work that is incomplete, your Inner Mentor will help you see that more effort is required, and it will do this in a supportive, encouraging way.

If you really are indulging in a dangerous way, your **Inner Controller** Mentor will remind you about it in a caring way. It will help you to devise a plan for controlling your appetites in a way that is flexible and realistic. It can help you find a venue where you can work with your Indulger part, discover the underlying needs that are triggering it, and change its behavior—perhaps a twelve-step program or an IFS therapist's office.

If you did something that went against your true values or caused harm that you regret, your **Guilt Tripper** Inner Mentor knows that it is important to take responsibility for your actions. It finds a supportive way to help you own up to your actions and their consequences. It helps you to make amends for what you did and set things right. If necessary, it helps you to work on and transform the parts of you that took those actions so they won't happen again. Your Inner Mentor does all of these things without making you feel bad about yourself.

If you tend to get into trouble because you ignore conventional ways of doing things, your **Molder** Inner Mentor can point this out in a caring way. If you have a Rebel part that needs to defy tradition just for the sake of defiance, your Inner Mentor can recognize this part and help you work with it to relax its extreme defiance so you can discover your true inner values.

If you are in a situation in which being visible could realistically be dangerous, your **Underminer** Inner Mentor can advise you of this from a rational place and help you decide how to handle the problem. If you are considering trying something that you may not succeed at because of your limitations, your Inner Mentor will help you to evaluate your potential without judgment. It will help you to be realistic about both your strengths and limitations and choose a way to step out into the world that will be satisfying.

Because the Destroyer tends to be so harmful, we haven't seen situations in which a **Destroyer** Inner Mentor is called for. What is needed is a strong Inner Champion (see chapter 10).

EXERCISE EVOKING YOUR INNER MENTOR

Think of a situation that tends to trigger your Inner Critic and that delivers some truth in its judgment of you. Respond to these prompts in your journal.

- The situation:
- What the Critic says to you:
- Evoke your Inner Champion, as we described in the last chapter, to support you in feeling better about yourself and knowing that you don't deserve to be treated in a harsh way. What does it say to you?
- Now think about how you would like your Inner Mentor to help you with the situation. Its input will usually be a paragraph of advice and ideas, not just a series of statements. What does it say to you?

Example

- Consider again if you were a mother whose Guilt Tripper Critic caused you to feel guilty about yelling at your daughter. Here's how you might complete this exercise.
- The situation: *Yelled at my daughter and upset her.*
- What the Critic says to you: *You are a horrible parent. How could you do that terrible thing to her? And you've done it so many times before. You are ruining her life!*
- Evoke your Inner Champion to support you in feeling better about yourself and knowing that you don't deserve to be treated in a harsh way. What does it say to you? *I know you're really a good mother. Everyone gets angry occasionally. You really love her and want the best for her. Pick up the pieces and move on from here.*
- Now think about how you would like your Inner Mentor to help you with the situation. What does it say to you? *I know that's not the way you want to treat your daughter, because you love her. Let's see what you can do to keep this from happening again. Your life has been very stressful lately, and you need to take better care of yourself. You could notice when you are starting to get angry with her and remember not to take it out on her. You could explore what's behind your anger, which may have nothing to do with her.*

THE CRITIC CLUSTER, CONTINUED

Figure 2 contains a full version of the Inner Critic cluster, including all the additional parts that have been introduced in this book.

- The **Inner Champion** supports you in being yourself and feeling good about yourself.

- The **Inner Mentor** supports you in working through problems that are preventing you from living your life the way you would like. It does this in a kind, helpful, encouraging way.

- The **Judge** criticizes other people, especially those who are criticizing you.

The Inner Champion is above the Inner Defender, because the Champion is a healthy version of the Defender. And the Inner Mentor is above the Inner Critic for the same reason. The Inner Champion and Inner Mentor are integrated, meaning that they work together to support you. The Judge is below the Inner Defender because both are polarized with the Inner Critic and both protect the Criticized Child.

Figure 2

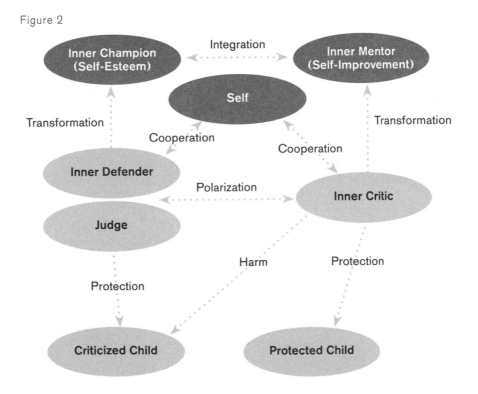

12

CRITICISM IN RELATIONSHIPS

You take your life in your own hands, and what
happens? A terrible thing: no one to blame.

ERICA JONG

So far, we have been exploring self-criticism by your Inner Critic and how
to transform it. However, criticism is also a major factor in most relationships, and many interpersonal problems are related to the Inner Critic.
This chapter looks at the situation in which your criticism is directed at someone
else and how your parts react when someone criticizes you.

THE JUDGE

Most of us are judgmental of other people more often than we think, even
if we don't necessarily express our judgments. Just stop and think how often
you compare yourself to others and find them lacking. In this book, we call
the part that criticizes others the *Judge* to distinguish it from the Inner Critic.
These parts are often similar—one judges you and one judges other people.
For some people, an Inner Critic might also be the part that turns its judgments on others.

People often become judgmental of others in order to protect their Criticized Child part. Something happens that triggers the pain of the Criticized Child. Maybe you feel rejected by someone, or perhaps you don't do well on a test or project. This prompts your Criticized Child to feel inadequate or worthless, and it may also trigger your Inner Critic to attack the Child. The Judge is a protector of the Child, so it may jump in and criticize the person who rejected you or the person who gave you the test, or even the entire educational system. If the Judge can prove that the other person is at fault, your Criticized Child doesn't have to feel bad. This strategy is also an attempt to counter the Critic's judgments of you; if the other person is bad, then you aren't. Thus, a criticism thrown at you by another person often boomerangs back at that person.

The Judge sometimes also comes forward to protect a different exile. Perhaps someone didn't give you the support you needed on a day when you were feeling sad. This brought up pain in one of your exiles, so you judged that person to keep from feeling this pain.

We're not saying that it is never valid to notice shortcomings in other people or to be discriminating about whom you want to spend time with. But the Judge often criticizes people to ward off our own underlying shame or self-attacks. The Judge can be just as harsh and punitive as the Inner Critic, and it can be just as painful for someone else to receive judgment from us as it is for us to receive it from our Inner Critic. In fact, this dynamic is a major factor in most relationship difficulties. Often both people are judging each other, triggering the pain of their exiles, and then protecting their exiles with more judgment, causing a vicious cycle of hurt feelings, arguments, and resentment.

REACTING TO AN OUTER CRITIC

When *another person* criticizes you, most of the parts in the Critic cluster tend to be triggered. Understanding what is happening will help you to work with these parts successfully and, therefore, respond in a more constructive way to criticism.

The Criticized Child gets activated because it believes the criticism and feels bad about itself.

The Inner Critic may become activated because it feels validated and thinks its job is to criticize you more. It may say, "See? I told you that you were no good. This proves it."

The part that we call the Inner Defender often gets triggered and attempts to protect the Child. But instead of just arguing with the Critic, it now also argues with the person who judged you in order to prove them wrong and exonerate the Child. It is now an Outer Defender as well.

The Judge may also get in on the act, supporting the Defender in protecting the Child. It says, "Not only is the judging person wrong, but it is actually their fault, not yours." This response will often trigger the other person's Criticized Child and then their Defender and Judge, making them criticize you more. You can see how this cycle could easily lead to a knockdown, drag-out fight. However, the more you have healed your Criticized Child and transformed your Critic, the less likely you are to get caught in such a situation.

CRISSY'S STORY

Crissy was a highly competent businesswoman who came into her therapy session and dissolved into tears. In five minutes she was furious, and shortly after, she was crying again. She had been confronted by someone whom she considered a good friend. The friend said that she was loud and bossy and that she didn't listen or show empathy. Crissy's Criticized Child part felt devastated and lost. Her Defender part wanted to lash out at the friend.

As we began to quiet things down and explore her dynamics in reaction to the occurrence, her story unfolded. She was raised Catholic and always attended religious school. Her family moved frequently, and she never had the opportunity for solid, age-appropriate socialization. At a young age, she entered a convent and spent the next ten years devoted to an order.

When she left, she became involved in business and was able to succeed because of her intelligence and hard work. Friendships had always been a little tricky. She thought that she was making progress toward developing friends and having more of a social circle.

When this friend confronted her, it activated all of the old critical voices that she had heard in childhood. The criticism from the friend triggered Crissy's Inner Critic, which said that she wasn't good enough, she wasn't interesting, and no one wanted to play with her. It reminded her of a time when she had moved into a new neighborhood and would try to walk to school with the girls on her block, who ran away to avoid her.

Crissy was able to get past the angry Defender and make some internal contact with her lonely little girl. This child part told her that all she wanted was to have a friend, a real friend. She (in Self) was able to become that friend for this child, and they went skipping down the street to school together. The child felt cared for and likable and, therefore, much better about herself.

In this healing process, Crissy was able to gain some perspective about her relationship with her adult friend. She developed a deeper understanding for her friend and was able to have some compassion for her. She also was able to look more realistically at her behavior that triggered the friend's criticism and decide if this was something she wanted to change in herself. But she could now do so with the help of a friendly, supportive Inner Mentor rather than the Inner Critic she had started with.

Remember, don't force your parts into the categories discussed here; get to know each part as a unique entity. For example, you might have three different parts that would be considered a Criticized Child. Each will be different from the others. Or you might have one part that is both a Defender and a Judge.

It is also worth remembering that you may react to someone even if they aren't judging you. All it takes is for your parts to *perceive* them as judging you. Or the other person may be mildly judging, and your parts may perceive them as being very harsh. Fights often start when minor acts of judgment lead to reactions, which trigger greater judgments, and around and around you go.

EXERCISE **THE PARTS TRIGGERED BY AN OUTER CRITIC**

- Think of a person who judges you and upsets your parts:
- Imagine that you are in a situation in which that person is criticizing you:
- What is the person is saying?

Notice how the person's words make you feel. You will probably be having more than one reaction. Focus on one of your reactions, access the part that is having that reaction, and get to know it briefly. Then answer whichever of the following questions are appropriate. Not all of them will be relevant for each part. And you may not have time to get to know the part well enough to answer all of them. Just do whatever you can.

Part:
- What type of part is it (e.g., Judge, Defender, protector, Criticized Child)?
- What does it feel?
- What is it trying to accomplish internally?
- What is it trying to accomplish externally?
- Which other part is it fighting with?
- Which other part is it protecting?

Then look for another feeling reaction, access that part, and get to know it, as above. Keep going until you have gotten to know each part that was triggered.

Example

Let's look at an example of how one of our clients did this exercise.

- Think of a person who judges you and upsets your parts: *My wife*
- Imagine that you are in a situation in which that person is criticizing you: *When I have forgotten to do something I said I would do or something important to her.*
- What is the person saying? *You never listen to me. You don't really care about me.*

Notice any parts that are having a reaction.

Part 1: *Little Joey*
- What type of part is it (e.g., Judge, Defender, protector, Criticized Child)? *Criticized Child*
- What does it feel? *Inadequate, not good enough.*

Part 2: *Shamer*
- What type of part is it (e.g., Judge, Defender, protector, Criticized Child)? *Critic*
- What does it feel? *Judgmental, annoyed.*
- What is it trying to accomplish internally? *Not sure*
- What is it trying to accomplish externally? *N/A*
- Which part is it fighting with? *Defender*
- Which part is it protecting? *Not sure*

Part 3: *Defender*
- What type of part is it (e.g., Judge, Defender, protector, Criticized Child)? *Inner Defender*
- What does it feel? *Angry*
- What is it trying to accomplish internally? *Defend against attacks from the Shamer.*
- What is it trying to accomplish externally? *Defend against the accusation from my wife.*
- Which part is it fighting with? *Shamer*
- Which part is it protecting? *Little Joey*

13

PERFECTIONISM

*Perfectionism is not a quest for the best. It is a pursuit of the
worst in ourselves, the part that tells us that nothing we do
will ever be good enough—that we should try again.*

JULIA CAMERON

I n this chapter and the next, we will apply what we have been learning to
two common Inner Critic issues—perfectionism and addictions. This chapter focuses on perfectionism. If you struggle with perfectionism, you have
extremely high standards for your behavior and especially for any products you
create, services you perform, or performances you give. With this pattern, you
may find that impending writing projects, reports, papers, or presentations
cause you a great deal of anxiety because you are so concerned about completing
them perfectly. You may consistently feel that your work isn't good enough and
that it must be improved before anyone else sees it.

With this pattern, you may doubt the quality of what you have produced by
focusing only on its possible shortcomings. By focusing only on your shortcomings, your Perfectionist Critic convinces you that your work isn't good enough
and must be improved before anyone sees it. The Perfectionist doesn't want you
to run the risk of appearing mediocre or even less than fabulous; you must be

perfect and flawless—a "ten"—to be OK. The result might be that you end up working much harder and longer on a project than is really necessary.

There may be a few situations in which you *need* to be perfect, or nearly so—for example, if you are proofreading or competing in gymnastics. But if you find yourself trying to be perfect much of the time or when it isn't really needed, this indicates perfectionism.

If you have this issue strongly, you may find you often are unable to turn in anything until you have reached the absolute deadline, or you may consistently turn in work late. You're likely to be afraid to finish a project because then you run the risk of exposing your shortcomings and being judged or, worse, ridiculed.

Your Perfectionist Inner Critic judges you harshly, saying that your efforts are "stupid," "lazy," or "sloppy." You hold these beliefs regardless of what other people say to the contrary. You might also have difficulty accepting others' praise of your work. Your Perfectionist Critic will focus entirely on what isn't perfect and fail to appreciate what you have done well.

A perfectionist pattern can also show up in concern over your appearance. You may believe you must be impeccably groomed and behave with perfect etiquette in all situations. You might strive to keep a flawlessly clean and beautiful house and even to have a perfect family. You might even strain to make perfect choices in every situation, believing any kind of mistake is unspeakable failure.

JEREMY'S STORY

Jeremy was always smart as a whip. As soon as you spent some time with him, it was clear. And if you hung around a little longer, you'd see that he was creative, artistic, and easily thought out of the box. Sounds like a ticket to success, right? Not quite.

Jeremy's midwestern family did not support his capacities. He wasn't a methodical toiler but was inclined to skip over parts of a project that weren't a challenge. He would often be able to get away with taking shortcuts, but sometimes his skipping steps led to results that were not up to par. His father was always strict and critical. He did not appreciate his son's creative genius. His interactions showed that he was as deeply disappointed in Jeremy as he was with his own life. They clashed over and over.

Jeremy moved away from home and began to get some better opportunities for success, based on his apparent talents. He wanted to please his bosses in Silicon Valley and prove how skilled he really was. He would take on a project and promise to delivery it by a certain deadline when deep inside he knew doing so would be impossible. He usually got close to finishing the job on time, but then his Perfectionist Inner Critic would kick in, saying it knew he could do better. He would work all night trying to make things perfect. This would lead to his coming in late or not showing up at work. His bosses thought he was lazy and not taking the job seriously. He was too afraid to ask for help or even give his superiors realistic progress reports. He worried that doing either would make him seem deficient. So he fell further and further behind and lost opportunity after opportunity, angering everyone around him in the process.

At the age of twenty-three, he was against a wall: he had enormous talent, a good deal of accumulated experience, but his work had ground to a halt. It was clear that Jeremy needed to make some peace with his perfectionism and take back control of his life.

Once Jeremy started doing IFS work, he learned that he had two critics: a Perfectionist and a Taskmaster. They worked in tandem to logjam his capacity to succeed at anything that he attempted. The Taskmaster wanted him to work hard and show the world (mainly his father) that he could achieve success with his skills by working in his own way. It pushed him to keep working and to make promises about what he would deliver without considering the reality. He was able to trace the origins of these patterns in his relationship with his father by exploring his memories of his childhood.

> Jeremy: Nothing I ever did seemed to be good enough for my father. No matter how hard I worked and what I produced, he tore me down and criticized everything I did. I now realize that I assumed I was going to fail regardless of how hard I worked, and I also see now that my father's approval was like a carrot always dangling in front of me—a lure that was always out of reach. Those emotions keep me in a pattern of promising an outrageously high level of performance that I can't ever live up to. They also keep me longing for something from my boss that I really wanted from my father.

The Perfectionist believed that he could always do better and was reluctant to allow him to show anyone any of his work along the way. It chided him and goaded him into redoing things again and again.

> Jeremy: I believe I need to completely wow my boss to earn my keep at work, so I'm always second-guessing my work and trying to figure out how to improve it. I'm afraid of turning in work because I expect to be criticized for it, and some part of me desperately seeks my boss's approval. I see now that I'm trying to avoid being judged as "less than" by my boss, which would reenact the dynamic with my father.

In his adult life, a part of him still believed that turning in work would make him an easy target for his boss's sharp criticism, so he found ways to avoid those deadlines altogether.

When Jeremy started working on these issues in therapy, he learned that his Perfectionist was, in fact, trying to protect him. It believed that if it forced him to make his work really perfect, he could prove to his boss that he was a success and deserved appreciation and love. Jeremy connected with his Perfectionist Critic and got permission to work with the young exile (wounded inner child part) it was protecting. He heard the child part's story about all the pain it felt from not getting his father's approval. Then Jeremy entered the scene with that part and gave it the love and appreciation it needed. He became the good father that the part needed. This child part ended up feeling relaxed and free and good about itself, which helped the Perfectionist Critic relax its need to push him constantly.

In Jeremy's case, his boss was reasonable, and his work was generally excellent, but he wasn't sure how much more needed to be done on a given job. He solved this problem by giving his boss feedback on his own work and asking for his boss's input. By doing this, he could determine when a project was good enough to turn in so he could move on to the next one. Jeremy was gradually able to set more realistic goals for himself at work. He learned that everyone wasn't like his father. His boss could be reasoned with and would support him when Jeremy set realistic goals and kept the boss informed about the status of his work. He began to get excellent reviews from his boss, and his career flourished.

Jeremy realized that he was behaving as if his boss were his father. He knew that although his father had been harsh and critical, his boss was a pretty nice guy who seemed fairly approachable when Jeremy wasn't in the grip of fear.

Jeremy: I did a reality check on the reactions I was expecting from my boss. I've seen him in a lot of different situations at work, and he's never flown off the handle like my father used to. I made a checklist of my fears, and I realized that none of them were going to happen with my boss—they were all about my father. I was playing an old tape over and over, and it was time to let it go. I asked my Perfectionist to see that my father was no longer a threat, and it agreed.

Jeremy also asked for a private meeting with his boss and explained that he wasn't clear about his boss's standards for his work. He asked if his boss would be willing to give him feedback about a project so he could find out where the bar was. He assured his boss that this information would go a long way toward helping him meet his deadlines. Jeremy's boss agreed to his request and was happy to see Jeremy taking initiative to resolve the problem.

> Jeremy: At first it was hard to talk to my boss, but I knew it was the only way out of my old pattern. I was never going to break the pattern unless I tried something different. It was really exciting to see that I could take initiative and create a different outcome. It helped me feel a lot more self-confidence.

Over time, Jeremy's boss communicated the standard of work he expected, and Jeremy learned that he didn't have to be perfect to do a good job. His fears died down as he discovered that his work was adequate. Also, even when his boss did express criticism, he did it in a respectful, professional manner that didn't threaten Jeremy.

14

ADDICTIONS

I wanted to write about the moment when your addictions no longer hide the truth from you. When your whole life breaks down. That's the moment when you have to somehow choose what your life is going to be about.

CHUCK PALAHNIUK

This chapter shows how to apply your understanding of Inner Critic work to the all-important topic of addictions, which includes not only alcohol, food, and drugs, but also other addictions, such as sex, shopping, and gambling.

An important dynamic around addictions is the relationship between the part that engages in the addiction and the Inner Critic part that tries to control the addiction. We call the addictive part the *Indulger* and the Inner Critic part the *Inner Controller*. These two parts are polarized, which means they are in conflict with each other. In this case, the conflict is about how much to indulge in the addiction.

The Inner Controller is concerned about the real-world consequences of your behavior (for example, becoming overweight, losing your job, alienating your friends, going broke). It may also be afraid of other people's judgments or rejection because of your behavior.

The Inner Controller tends to be rigid and punitive. It usually has fixed and precise standards for how you should live. It may have an opinion about exactly how much you should eat or drink, how you express your sexuality, how you spend money, or how you engage in other activities that might not serve you or might get you in trouble. It tries to control your behavior in these areas by telling you what to do and criticizing you whenever you overstep or ignore its rules. As long as you follow its dictates, it won't judge you, but if you get out of line, then it attacks.

There are two problems with the Inner Controller: The first is that its standards are often too extreme and rigid. The second is that it tries to enforce these standards by attacking and shaming you when you fail to measure up to them.

The Inner Controller is in conflict with the Indulger, which habitually over-indulges in food, drink, sex, gambling, shopping, gaming, relationships, thrill seeking, online activities, or anything else that can be harmful if taken to excess. This part goes to extremes in an effort to keep down the pain of parts of you that could be needy, frightened, ashamed, or grieving. It is a protector that is often trying to soothe or numb underlying feelings of pain or need through food or drugs or alcohol. Or it may try to distract you from these feelings through shopping, gambling, or thrill-seeking behavior.

The Indulger may also engage in addiction in order to suppress feelings of anger or assertive behavior that it thinks is unacceptable or dangerous. There are a wide variety of emotions and behaviors that can be soothed or suppressed by addictive or indulgent behavior. The Indulger may make you a true addict, or it may only lead you to indulge in food, drink, sex, or something else to an extent that might not be considered addictive, but still causes problems in your life. Maybe you aren't an alcoholic, but your drinking is still excessive and causes problems. Maybe you aren't obese, but you still struggle with overeating and shame about the way you look. Maybe you aren't a true shopping or gambling addict, but you still keep yourself in financial trouble.

The Inner Controller and Indulger are constantly engaged in a power struggle inside you. Sometimes they are battling it out when you are in a position to indulge—for example, when you're in front of the fridge at night or at a bar with friends. At other times, the Inner Controller takes over for a while, and you are very careful with your diet or drinking, for example. Then the Indulger takes over, and you go on an eating binge or a bender. Then afterward, the Inner Controller takes back control and shames you unmercifully for overdoing it.

The Inner Controller truly wants to do what's best for you, but it goes about this in a harsh, punitive way that doesn't work and causes a lot of pain. Your

Inner Controller may have learned this strategy by modeling itself after the way your parents tried to control you as a child.

When the Inner Controller attacks you after an indulgence, the Criticized Child is the part of you that receives the brunt of the attacks. It feels very bad about the indulging that has happened. It feels ashamed, inadequate, and deeply flawed. The Criticized Child often promises to do better, but the very presence of the shame often triggers the Indulger to engage in binge eating, excessive drinking, and other out-of-control behaviors in order to block the shame.

The Inner Controller may be present even if your current habits are not out of line. You may feel as though you are fighting a chronic battle with someone who does not see or know who you are today—a part that thinks it must control you even when there is really minimal danger. However, in this chapter, we will focus on situations in which the Indulger is indeed engaging in destructive behavior and there is a realistic concern about that behavior being out of control.

In addition to the Indulger, a defiant part, *the Rebel,* may get triggered. The Rebel doesn't want to let other people control you, and it even will defy other parts of you, especially the Inner Controller, that may be trying to control you. It may purposely engage in the addictive or indulgent behavior just to prove that it can't be pushed around. The Rebel is trying to make sure that you have your autonomy, but it goes overboard, making it difficult for you to cooperate with other people or to have internal harmony.

Thus, the Inner Controller's strategy often backfires and leads to a more extreme expression of the behavior it is trying to stop. In fact, sometimes its punitive attempts to control can create a problem where there isn't one or make a minor problem much worse.

Though the Inner Controller and the Indulger are polarized and in conflict about your indulgent behavior, the Rebel is even more at war with the Controller, because it is concerned not only about being free to indulge, but also about having its autonomy and not being dominated by the Controller.

OVERCOMING YOUR ADDICTION

Most people think that if only the Inner Controller could be completely in charge, the Indulger couldn't act out, and everything would be just fine. However, the irony is that the more stringent the Controller is, the stronger the Indulger and the Rebel become. Or if the Inner Controller is able to stay in charge, it becomes so rigid and ascetic that it doesn't leave you enough space to be in touch with your sensuality and freedom and to enjoy the pleasures of life.

It is too afraid that if it allowed you to do these things, you would slip back into addiction. And in some cases, it is right.

So in order to fully resolve this problem, you must heal and transform both the Inner Controller and the Indulger. Let's look at the Indulger first.

You must get in contact with the exiles that the Indulger is trying to protect and heal them, using the IFS steps outlined in chapters 3 through 8. Then the Indulger will be able to relax and let go of its addictive tendencies. Keep in mind that there is often more than one exile that is being soothed or suppressed by the Indulger, and usually all of them must be healed before it will let go.

In addition, the Indulger might be trying to stop you from being angry or aggressive, especially if you have a food addiction. In this case, you will have to explore what makes the Indulger afraid of these feelings and behaviors. From Self, you can befriend the Indulger, reassure it about its fears, and ask if it would be willing to give up or change its role, in the same way you did the Critic. You might also need to heal the Inner Child it is protecting. Your anger may need to become less extreme, and the Indulger may have to learn that a certain amount of anger and strength is fine.

The aim of your work with the Indulger is to transform it so you can have the healthy capacity of *conscious consumption,* where you are free to enjoy the pleasures of life, but you don't need to go overboard with them because you are truly after pleasure and not soothing or blocking underlying pain.

The aim of working with the Inner Controller is to get it to let go of its rigid standards and allow you to have healthy sensuality and pleasure in your life. The Inner Controller is probably also protecting some exiles, so they will also need to be healed for it to fully let go. For example, if you were ridiculed by your peers for being fat as a child, your Inner Controller will be trying to protect you from the shame that is carried by an exile from those times.

It is also useful to develop an Inner Champion that supports your right to have the healthy capacity of sensuality and aliveness. In the process, you can transform your Inner Controller into an Inner Mentor that can help you with the moderation you need in your life without being harsh and judgmental.

While the Inner Controller and Indulger/Rebel are polarized with each other, the healthy capacities of moderation and sensuality naturally integrate with each other, so that you can have both at the same time.

It is also sometimes useful to have a dialogue between the Inner Controller and either the Indulger or the Rebel to help resolve their polarization—the way they fight with each other instead of cooperating. You can moderate this dialogue from Self and work with these parts to encourage them to listen to each other and work together for your good rather than trying to overcome each other. You work with them just the way a mediator works with two people who are in conflict. (See Jay's book *Resolving Inner Conflict* for more details about how to work through polarization.)

BRENDA'S STORY

Bonnie writes: When I started work with Brenda, she framed her whole life history in terms of her weight. "I weighed 123 when I graduated from high school, then freshman year in college I blew up to 145. In my junior year, I had a great boyfriend and I got down to 120. Then we broke up and I graduated from college at 150. After my dad died I was up to 175, then I dieted down to 138 by the time I got married. Then after my first child I was up to 170 again."

Brenda struggled with compulsive eating issues throughout her life. She saw herself and her value through the lens of the scale.

Before coming to IFS therapy, she described her system as being like a big pizza pie divided in half. On one side were the addicts and on the other were the controllers and critics. On each side, she had named a number of parts that she could recognize. To her great dismay, she was not able to make much headway in changing her system.

"One of my big challenges around compulsive eating is my addiction to sugar," she said. "I have a part I call *my Rebellious Teen,* who wakes me up in the middle of the night, takes the keys to the car, and drives to the local 7-Eleven to buy Ring Dings and Mallomars. This part goes out and eats whatever it wants. There is no stopping it.

"Then, the Inner Critic part, called *the Big J,* kicks in and tells me what an idiot and a loser I am. I know the Big J's intentions are good, because it is trying to stop me from overeating." The Big J was very concerned about her being overweight and, therefore, unattractive. It pushed her so hard because it wanted her to be attractive to men and find love in her life. Brenda added, "But it makes me feel so worthless. And the Big J's attacks really don't stop the eating for very long."

Using our terminology, the Big J is an Inner Controller Critic, and the Rebellious Teen is an Indulger and Rebel. They are polarized with each other over how much Brenda should eat.

In her IFS work, Brenda was able to gain some distance from these parts and more easily dialogue with them. As she got to know the Big J, she saw that it was modeled on her father. He would tell her that she had too much of her mother in her. He felt she was too strong and bossy. So the Big J judged her about these things, as well as her eating.

One of the reasons Brenda overate was to soothe herself and quiet her natural energy, so she wouldn't be strong and activate the wrath of the Big J. Notice the incredible irony. The Big J was unknowingly triggering a part of her that ate too much, the very thing it is trying to stop her from doing. This is a common occurrence with parts.

As I worked with Brenda, she was able to access the Little Girl part of her who felt her father's disapproval for being outgoing and smart like her mother. She made contact with the Little Girl from a loving place of Self. Brenda entered those scenes with her father and protected the Little Girl from him. She reassured the Little Girl that she was fine just as she is, and it was OK for her to be strong and smart. She took her out of that harmful childhood situation and brought her to a safe place in her current home, where she wouldn't be criticized any more.

Then we checked with the Rebellious Teen. Over time, it began to relax its need to binge since it didn't need to soothe the Little Girl any more. Brenda's eating became regularized. She said, "I now eat when I am hungry, and I don't binge any more. The eating comes mostly from my Self."

After a while, she checked in with the Big J, and it was pretty relaxed since she wasn't overeating much. As she lost weight, it got more and more quiet. Brenda said, "By now, I can even give myself permission to have some treats when I want them without the Big J lambasting me. Now I see myself more in terms of my worth as a person, not just my weight.

"Another thing I took away from this work was seeing that in my pizza-pie system, my parts were all protectors, and the Self was missing." When she got in touch with the Self through our IFS work, it took on a whole new power and meaning.

Six months after therapy ended, Brenda said, "What has stayed with me is the capacity to go back to Self whenever I start to hear the Critic or feel impulsive. I can access its power and wisdom and find my ground again."

15

GENDER AND THE INNER CRITIC

The first problem for all of us, men and women, is not to learn, but to unlearn.

GLORIA STEINEM

Our Inner Critic messages are strongly influenced by a host of cultural factors—gender, race, religion, ethnicity, sexual orientation, socioeconomic class, and so on. Women's Inner Critics, for example, are more likely to judge them about their bodies and sexual attractiveness, while men's tend to judge them about their worldly success. People who break away from the religion or national identity of their childhood will often have an Inner Critic that judges them for that transgression and attempts to bring them back into the fold. People of color and various sexual orientations often have to cope with Critics that echo society's prejudices.

Hal and Sidra Stone, in their book *Embracing Your Inner Critic,* talk about the Inner Patriarchy as a "powerful ally of the Inner Critic in women." They define the Inner Patriarch as "the inner representation of the outer societal beliefs in the inferiority of women, and it echoes all the judgments of women that are prevalent in our culture."[1] They believe that women suffer more acutely than men from Inner Critic issues as a result of years of patriarchal thinking. Women believe they need to "improve" and please others just to level the playing field.

Two-and-a-half times as many women as men have taken our Inner Critic questionnaire, confirming the Stones' experience that more women than men consciously struggle with their Inner Critics. Of the respondents, women rated their difficulties with their Critics slightly higher than men for all seven types, and more so for the Molder and Underminer Critics. These are just preliminary findings; we will be studying further how people's Critics are distributed over the seven types.

CHANGES IN GENDER ATTITUDES

We won't try to cover much of the broad scope of sociocultural issues in this short chapter; we will mainly focus on our knowledge of how recent changes in attitudes about gender have affected the content of Inner Critic attacks in the populations we are familiar with.

The revolution in gender roles over the past forty years has blasted open expectations for many men and women. We have noticed that we, our clients, and our friends have a larger sense of our potentials. Our deeply held beliefs about the roles we can play and the satisfactions we are allowed have been challenged. Many women can now see themselves exerting their strength and influence in previously unimagined arenas—career ambition, professional position, corporate management, political influence, activist and nonprofit leadership, and media visibility. They are now allowed to tap into their desire for authority and power without being ashamed of exerting leadership and showing competence.

Many men, on the other hand, are interested in being more personally open, communicative, and in touch with their feelings, or their partners are challenging them to be that way. Men with families are now asked to be responsible on the home front—sharing child-care responsibilities, being on the food-prep rotation, and being attentive to their partner's emotional needs. Today, a young married couple might take for granted that the man may leave work early to pick up the kids so the woman can work late or make a big presentation to a client in another city.

BONNIE'S STORY

Bonnie writes: The type of Critic I have struggled with most is the Guilt Tripper. I come by it naturally because of my Jewish heritage. It judges me for not being enough—not for lacking capacity, but for not being fully present and attentive.

If I am focused on one thing—my work, my garden, my spiritual development, my current craft project—there is always something I am neglecting.

I am a woman of the sixties generation, whose possibilities exploded out of the women's movement. The emotional challenge of that time for me was to balance the excitement of a real career with the desire to be a wife and mother—and then the desire to be a successful single mom. Whenever I focused on one of those options, I felt that I should be attending to the other. When I was working, I felt as though I should be with my daughter, and when I was with her, there were career tasks and stimulating challenges that distracted me. I was pulled by travel and the exploration of spiritual issues, which opened and deepened me but did not settle me down during those years.

My Guilt Tripper manifests in a pair of regular dreams, one usually following the other. In the first dream, I am about to graduate from college, and I realize that I have not finished a civics course. All term I have been meaning to talk to the professor but haven't gotten around to it. On the day of the final, I realize, to my great dismay, that I don't even know where the classroom is. I feel foolish and guilty that I have not taken care of this responsibility properly.

In the second dream, I am walking the streets of New York City with my beautiful five-year-old daughter. She is carrying a box of jewelry with chains dribbling out the sides. I decide to leave her with a group of strangers in order to go to an important meeting. Halfway there, on the subway, I think, "Maybe that wasn't such a great idea." I feel guilty about not paying proper attention to my role as a parent.

WOMEN

Bonnie writes: Expanded roles for many women I know have brought with them conflicting expectations, both internal and external. Now there is a whole smorgasbord of things that we can feel lacking in. Before, we were limited to having a clean house; perfect children; a sexy body; a patient, supportive attitude toward our husbands; and the best cake at the bake sale. The sad story is that those expectations haven't really gone away. Added to them are having a career that brings in a substantial income, being facile with new technology, being up to date on current events, and making intelligent conversation with colleagues.

We now have an increasing abundance of reasons to put ourselves down and more areas in which our Inner Critics may judge us. When focusing our attention on one of these areas, we often feel guilty that our scorecard shows us to be below par in another. We can drive ourselves shamelessly in one arena, egged on by a Perfectionist Critic that compares us to our sisters and always finds someone who is doing more, doing it more easily, or looking better while doing it! We have many things higher on the priority list than ourselves and therefore must find ways to keep our basic needs in check. An Inner Critic attack is one great way to do this; it makes us feel small and unworthy.

The conflicting internal struggle about whether to put one's self out in the world is heightened by the plethora of possibilities. It is harder to hide behind that proverbial white picket fence and say, "I'm just a mom." We can no longer say, "I'm just a woman. I don't know things like that." Everyone knows that we could be doing more. There are no more excuses. This triggers the part of us that fears we are inadequate little girls going off to work in the big world in Mommy's clothing, and it activates an Underminer Critic that says we'll never be good enough.

It is my hope that identifying the seven types of Inner Critics will contribute to women being able to get space from self-judgment and experience a new kind of liberation.

MEN

Jay writes: Many men I know also have new things to struggle with. Our avenues for deficiency and vulnerability to attack have also expanded. Now we may be expected to be aware of home and family issues, open in love relationships, and good in bed. These are new areas for Inner Critic attacks. Men with young families may have to know the soccer schedule and the names of all their children's teachers. They may need to manage their careers while being more on call for family schedule shifts.

Meanwhile, the old places of vulnerability to self-judgment are as prevalent as ever. Men are still expected to be successful, worldly, confident, masculine, powerful, and wealthy. And there is often an Inner Critic just waiting to judge us if we fall down in any of these areas—or worse yet, a Critic that constantly attacks us for never being adequate. This is often the Taskmaster or the Perfectionist.

CONCLUSION

LIVING FREE OF YOUR INNER CRITICS

We cannot give any reason for the fact that we love being ourselves.
We can come up with reasons, but none of them will be true because there
aren't any; we just inherently love ourselves and our nature. And in our True
Nature, we love everything and everybody. That love is simply part of reality.

A. H. ALMAAS
The Unfolding Now

When you have worked with your Inner Critic parts and your Criticized Child parts enough that they are healed and transformed, what will your life be like? What is it like to be free of your Inner Critics?

There is an amazing reinforcing quality that happens when you walk away from old patterns of self-hatred. Like when you take the first tentative steps on stones across a stream, you find your footing and dance lightly ahead. You no longer have to rely on the tattered net of old beliefs to hold you. Your safety net becomes a new fabric of self-confidence and self-love woven from inner support, experiences of successful living, and your growing capacities.

One of the participants in our Inner Critic Class said, "I learned that while my Inner Critic can give me harsh messages to shy away from situations, she really means to protect me from my personal pain, fear, and grief. So I embrace her. And, separate from that harsh voice, there is the centered *me,* who can experience the painful feelings of my parts and care for them."

The most important result of being free from your Critic is that you feel good about yourself. A natural sense of being valuable fills your consciousness. You walk taller and feel self-confident, capable, lovable, and good. You know you are worthwhile; you believe that you deserve appreciation and respect just for being yourself, not because you have done something to earn it. You understand that you don't have to accomplish something or be someone. It's not about the externals—you don't have to be smart, caring, or beautiful. You are valuable just for being you.

Many of our clients report that they learn to appreciate themselves. They feel good about their personal strengths, talents, and skills. They value their accomplishments and the ways they have grown. They appreciate what they have to offer to other people, and they see this self-worth reflected in how people respond to them.

When you are free of your Inner Critic, you accept yourself just as you are, including any limitations or problems. Your Inner Mentor helps you to be aware of your shortcomings without judgment. We are all works in progress. When you unconditionally accept yourself, it is easier to look at your issues because you don't judge yourself for them. You can hold up a mirror to look honestly at yourself because you don't have a Critic breathing down your neck. When changes are needed, creative solutions appear in intuitive ways. You have the inner support to take the risk to do things differently without any nagging self-judgment.

Most people find that, as they begin to change, they develop a palpable sense of confidence and inner trust. They walk forward without constantly looking over their shoulders or wasting time rehashing and regretting things they have said or done. They sense that their Inner Mentor is there to guide them in a kind, caring, accepting way. It becomes a real force in their lives. They develop a rhythm of knowing what to do and having the courage to follow through. This becomes a fallback position that they can count on.

Since you can be guided by your Inner Mentor, you can move more fluidly toward becoming the person you want to be. Sometimes moving forward does involve doing the things an Inner Critic might want you to do. You can work hard and produce excellence. You have integrity and care about other people; you are moderate in your appetites. You don't take unnecessary risks; you can appreciate tradition and follow convention when called for. The difference is that you can do all these things without needing to be pushed or judged by a Critic.

And you don't overdo them. You don't overwork or put yourself on a rigid diet, for example. You can choose to take these actions when a situation calls for them and only to the degree they are needed. When you make decisions in this way, they have an energy and an authenticity that put music in your step and draws other people toward your light. Your life is balanced, which makes it smoother and more fun.

Of course, this is an ideal picture we have just painted. As you transform your Critic parts, you will move toward this condition while not necessarily reaching it completely. After all, you don't have to be perfect.

IFS is a very powerful method for transforming your Inner Critic. We hope this book has made a significant difference in your internal landscape around self-esteem as well as in your life. We recommend that you use IFS for help with other psychological issues you may have.

GLOSSARY

Accessing a part Tuning in to a part experientially, through an image, an emotion, a body sensation, or internal dialogue, so you can work with the part using IFS.

Activation A situation in which a part has been triggered by an event or person so that it influences your feelings and actions.

Blending The situation in which a part has taken over your consciousness, so that you feel its feelings, believe its attitudes are true, and act according to its impulses. Blending is a more extreme form of activation.

Burden A painful emotion or negative belief about yourself or the world, which a part has taken on as the result of a past harmful situation or relationship, usually from childhood.

Concerned part A part that feels judgmental or angry toward the part you are focused on. When you are blended with a concerned part, you aren't in Self.

Conscious blending The situation in which you choose to feel a part's emotions because doing so will be helpful in the IFS process. You are aware that you are blended and can unblend easily if necessary.

Criticized Child An exile who believes the judgments of the Inner Critic and feels ashamed, worthless, not valuable, guilty, self-doubting, or inadequate. It is both harmed and activated by the Critic.

Defender A protector that argues with people who judge you and that tries to prove that you are valuable and didn't do anything wrong. See also "Inner Defender."

Destroyer A type of Critic that makes pervasive attacks on your fundamental self-worth. It is deeply shaming and tells you that you shouldn't exist.

Exile A young child part that is carrying pain from the past.

Extreme part A part that has a dysfunctional or problematic role because it carries a burden from the past or because a protector is trying to protect an exile.

Guilt Tripper A type of Critic that attacks you for some specific action you took (or didn't take) in the past that was harmful to someone, especially someone you care about. It might also attack you for violating a deeply held value. It constantly makes you feel bad and will never forgive you.

Healthy role A role that is the natural function of a part when it has no burdens. A healthy part is a part that has a healthy role.

Inner Champion An aspect of your Self that supports and encourages you and helps you feel good about yourself. It is the magic bullet for dealing with the negative impact of the Inner Critic.

Inner Controller A type of Critic that tries to control impulsive behavior, such as overeating, getting enraged, using drugs, or engaging in other addictions. It shames you after you binge or use. It is usually in a constant battle with an impulsive part.

Inner Critic A protector that judges you, demeans you, and pushes you to do things. It makes you feel bad about yourself.

Inner Defender A protector that tries to argue with the Critic and prove that you are worthwhile.

Inner Mentor The healthy version of the Critic. It encourages you to look at yourself with humility to see the ways in which you need to change how you operate in the world, and it helps you to make these changes in a supportive, encouraging way.

Judge A protector that judges other people, often to protect your Criticized Child.

Legacy burden A burden that a part takes on from a parent who had that burden.

Molder A type of Critic that tries to get you to fit a certain societal mold or act in a certain way that is based on your own family or cultural mores. It attacks you when you don't fit and praises you when you do.

Part A subpersonality, which has its own feelings, perceptions, beliefs, motivations, and memories.

Perfectionist A type of Critic that tries to get you to do everything perfectly. This part has very high standards for behavior, performance, and production. When you don't meet its standards, the Perfectionist attacks you by saying that your work or behavior isn't good enough.

Positive intent The laudable reason a part has taken on a role. All parts are playing their roles in an attempt to help you or protect you, even if the effect of the role is negative.

Protected Child The exile that is being protected by the Inner Critic. It may be the same as or different from the Criticized Child.

Protector A part that tries to block pain that is arising inside you or to protect you from hurtful incidents or distressing relationships in your current life.

Rebel A part that defies an Inner Critic by refusing to do what the Critic wants.

Reparenting The step in the IFS process in which the Self gives an exile what it needs to feel better or to change a harmful childhood situation.

Retrieval The step in the IFS process in which the Self takes an exile out of a harmful childhood situation and into a place where it can be safe and comfortable.

Role The job that a part performs to help you. It may be primarily internal, or it may involve the way the part interacts with people and acts in the world.

Self The core aspect of you that is your true self, your spiritual center. The Self is relaxed, open, and accepting of yourself and others. It is curious, compassionate, calm, and interested in connecting with other people and your parts.

Self-leadership The situation in which your parts trust you, in Self, to make decisions and take action in your life.

Taskmaster A type of Critic that tries to get you to work hard in order to be successful. It attacks you and tells you that you are lazy, stupid, or incompetent in order to motivate you. It often gets into a battle with a part that procrastinates in order to avoid work.

Unblending Separating from a part that is blended with you, so that you can be in Self.

Unburdening The step in the IFS process in which the Self helps an exile to release its burdens through an internal ritual.

Underminer A type of Critic that tries to undermine your self-confidence and self-esteem so you won't take risks where you might fail. It may also try to prevent you from getting too big, powerful, or visible in order to avoid the threat of attack and rejection.

Witnessing The step in the IFS process in which the Self witnesses the childhood origin of a part's burdens.

NOTES

INTRODUCTION

1. Although many people have tremendous success using our self-therapy approach, others will see more progress with the additional support of a trained psychotherapist. If you do need a therapist, IFS practitioners are available in most locations to help. If you are in the midst of a major life crisis, it's always a good idea to seek help. See "Resources" for information on finding an IFS therapist.

1. GETTING TO KNOW YOUR INNER CRITIC

1. You can also take this questionnaire on our website, PsycheMaps: Tools in Support of IFS Growth Programs (psychemaps.com).

3. COMING INTO SELF: UNBLENDING FROM YOUR CRITIC AND CHILD

1. If you are still unable to get the Criticized Child to unblend, then you probably need more help with this work than you can get from this book. You could read our book *Self-Therapy,* take one of our Inner Critic or IFS classes, or go into IFS therapy. See "Resources" for more information.

4. BECOMING OPEN TO YOUR CRITIC: UNBLENDING FROM YOUR INNER DEFENDER

1. The Inner Defender and the Inner Critic are fighting over whether or not you (the Criticized Child) should feel bad about yourself or OK. This is an example of *polarization,* an important concept in IFS. It refers to a situation in which two parts are in conflict with each other. They are fighting with each other over what you should feel or how you should act.

2. If you try all these suggestions and the Defender still won't step aside, you may need additional support with your Inner Critic work. See "Resources" for suggestions.

3. Remember, each of your parts is unique and has its own unique characteristics. Even though we are using category names for parts, such as *Inner Critic, Criticized Child,* and *Inner Defender,* please call your parts by whatever names seem right.

5. BEFRIENDING YOUR INNER CRITIC

1. If your Inner Critic still won't answer your questions, you might need more help with this work than you can get from this book. See "Resources" for suggestions.

6. UNCOVERING THE ORIGINS OF YOUR CRITICIZED CHILD

1. If you are still unable to get permission to work with your Child, you probably need more help with this work than you can get from this book. See "Resources" for suggestions.

2. After following these suggestions, if you are still unable to get the Child or a concerned part to unblend, you probably need more support with this work than you can get from this book. If you run into trouble at a later point in your work with the Child, you might also need more help. See "Resources" for suggestions.

7. HEALING YOUR INNER CHILDREN

1. Help Sheet 2 includes step 8, "Releasing the Critic," which is described in the next chapter.

9. TRANSFORMING AN INNER CRITIC WITH A LEGACY BURDEN

1. This is the IFS technique called *updating.*

15. GENDER AND THE INNER CRITIC

1. Hal and Sidra Stone, *Embracing Your Inner Critic* (San Francisco: Harper San Francisco, 1993), 93.

RESOURCES

IFS THERAPISTS

If you want to find an IFS therapist to work with, consult the website of the Center for Self-Leadership, the official IFS organization: selfleadership.org. It contains a listing of IFS-certified therapists, which can be searched by geographical location. Some of these therapists, including us, offer IFS sessions by telephone.

INNER CRITIC AND IFS CLASSES AND GROUPS

We teach classes for the general public on using IFS to work with the Inner Critic. They can be taken by telephone or in person in the San Francisco Bay Area. Each class is either a six-week course or a weekend workshop. We also offer classes in which people learn to use IFS for self-help and peer counseling, and classes on other psychological issues, such as overeating and procrastination.

We also offer ongoing IFS groups and classes, including groups and classes that meet over the telephone. See our website, IFS Growth Programs (personal-growth-programs.com), for more information and a schedule of classes and groups.

IFS BOOKS AND AUDIO PRODUCTS

Self-Therapy: A Step-by-Step Guide to Creating Wholeness and Healing Your Inner Child Using IFS, by Jay Earley (Larkspur, CA: Pattern System Books, 2009). Shows how to do IFS sessions on your own or with a partner. Also a manual of the IFS method that can be used by therapists. Bonnie has produced a card deck based on the illustrations in this book. See our website, IFS Growth Programs (personal-growth-programs.com).

Resolving Inner Conflict: Working Through Polarization Using Internal Family Systems Therapy, by Jay Earley (Larkspur, CA: Pattern System Books, 2009). A professional book on how to work with polarization.

IFS Basic Course and *IFS Exiles Course.* Two recorded courses that teach you how to use IFS to work on your personal issues.

Introduction to the Internal Family System Model, by Richard Schwartz (Oak Park, IL: Trailheads Publications, 2001). A basic introduction to parts and IFS for clients and potential clients.

Internal Family Systems Therapy, by Richard Schwartz (New York: Guilford Press, 1997). The primary professional book on IFS and a must-read for therapists.

The Mosaic Mind: Empowering the Tormented Selves of Child Abuse Survivors, by Richard Schwartz and Regina Goulding (Oak Park, IL: Trailheads Publications, 2003). A professional book on using IFS with trauma, especially sexual abuse.

You Are the One You've Been Waiting For: Bringing Courageous Love to Intimate Relationships, by Richard Schwartz (Oak Park, IL: Center for Self Leadership, 2008). A popular book providing an IFS perspective on intimate relationships. To purchase Schwartz's books, visit the IFS store at the Center for Self Leadership website (selfleadership.org).

INNER CRITIC BOOKS AND AUDIO PRODUCTS

All of the following are available on our website, IFS Growth Programs (personal-growth-programs.com).

Companion Workbook for Freedom from Your Inner Critic, by Jay Earley and Bonnie Weiss. A compilation of all the exercises in this book, with space for writing out answers. Download it for free from our website.

Illustrated Inner Critic Workbook: Exploring the 7 Types of Inner Critics and Their Champions, by Bonnie Weiss. A graphic support for understanding some of the basic IFS and Inner Critic concepts. Contains illustrations and fill-in-the-blank questions. Suitable for classes, adolescents, and individual clients.

Activating Your Inner Champion Instead of Your Inner Critic: Transforming Self-Criticism into Self-Esteem, by Jay Earley and Bonnie Weiss (Larkspur, CA: Pattern System Books, 2012). This book, which contains detailed descriptions of each of the seven Inner Critics, links to an online quiz and profiling program. You can create a profile of each Critic, including what it says to you, what it looks like, the typical situations that tend to activate it, and its motivations. It also allows you to profile an Inner Champion for you in response to each of the seven Critics—what it says to nurture you, guide you, help you plan actions, and set boundaries for your Inner Critic. With this profile you can specify what you want your personal Champion to say to you and what it looks like, from each of its four ways of helping you, as discussed in chapter 10. You can print out your profiles or keep them on a web workbook, so you can use them in a daily practice for activating your Inner Champion to support you whenever your Inner Critic starts attacking.

Inner Critic/Inner Champion Guided Meditations. Recorded meditations for working with Inner Critics and activating Inner Champions.

IFS Demonstration Sessions with Inner Critics. Recordings of actual therapy sessions facilitated by Jay and Bonnie that show how to work with Inner Critic parts using IFS.

Transforming Perfectionism. A multimedia course that describes in detail how to transform a Perfectionist Critic using IFS.

We are publishing short books on some of the seven types of Critics. These will allow us to go into much more detail on each of them—how they operate, their motives, their origins, how to work with them, and exercises for evoking their Inner Champions. So far we have published *Letting Go of Perfectionism* and *Taking Action: Working Through Procrastination and Achieving Your Goals.*

ARTICLES AND APPLICATIONS

Our website, IFS Growth Programs (personal-growth-programs.com), contains popular and professional articles on IFS and its application to various psychological issues, and more are being added all the time. You can also sign up for our email list to receive future articles and notification of upcoming classes and groups.

Jay is working on a web application for self-therapy, which will be available in September 2013.

THE PATTERN SYSTEM

In this book, we have explored the cluster of parts and healthy capacities that emerge in response to the Inner Critic and the issues around self-criticism and self-esteem. This is one dimension in the Pattern System, which is a way of understanding your personality and mapping the human psyche that can lead directly to psychological healing and personal growth.

There is also a dimension of the Pattern System for each of the seven types of Inner Critics. Each dimension includes the Critic, a part that is related to the Critic, a part that can be polarized with the Critic, a particular type of Criticized Child, and two healthy capacities that are supported by the Inner Champion and Mentor for that dimension.

You can explore the Pattern System in more detail on the website, the Pattern System (patternsystem.com). Jay is publishing a series of books on individual patterns and also plans a number of books that cover the system as a whole.

ACKNOWLEDGMENTS

We are deeply grateful to Dick Schwartz for creating such a brilliant method of therapy, Internal Family Systems Therapy (IFS), which makes it possible to profoundly change people's Inner Critics. We have learned so much about the human psyche and about Inner Critics from our therapy clients, group members, and the students in our IFS and Inner Critic classes, as well as the participants in the IFS training programs we have helped to lead. We received additional help from those people who volunteered to read early versions of some of the chapters and provide feedback, and also those who were the guinea pigs for the first versions of the Inner Critic questionnaire and profile program.

Stefanie Weiss helped us think through the early stages of the book and edited part of the manuscript. Amy Rost has done an excellent job of editing and putting into shape this new, expanded version of the book. Ed Hinkelman and Gayle Madison helped us birth the ideas that led to our Inner Critic questionnaire. We deeply appreciate the ongoing support and holding of our IFS community group. Special thanks go to Joan Slater and Mindy Lamberson, whose creative input supported the unfolding of this work.

Marla Silverman has been the inexhaustible champion of this work. She has been there all the way through, reading every chapter, listening to new ideas, and providing feedback whenever we needed it. George Silverman suggested the great term *Inner Champion* for us to use.

Kathy Wilber has done an excellent job on the programming for our Inner Critic questionnaire and profile program. Riley Miller and Jaime Becker have focused their keen eyes on the project.

ABOUT THE AUTHORS

J ay Earley, PhD, is a psychologist, psychotherapist, group leader, teacher, supervisor, trainer, and theorist who has been practicing psychotherapy for forty years, currently in the San Francisco Bay Area. His books include *Self-Therapy, Resolving Inner Conflict, Working with Anger in IFS, Embracing Intimacy,* and *Interactive Group Therapy.*

Bonnie Weiss, M.A., LCSW, is a psychotherapist, teacher, supervisor, trainer, and coach who has been practicing since 1974, currently in the San Francisco Bay Area. She is the author of the *Illustrated Inner Critic Workbook* and the audio products *IFS Courses, IFS Guided Meditations,* and *IFS Demonstration Sessions.*

ABOUT SOUNDS TRUE

Sounds True is a multimedia publisher whose mission is to inspire and support personal transformation and spiritual awakening. Founded in 1985 and located in Boulder, Colorado, we work with many of the leading spiritual teachers, thinkers, healers, and visionary artists of our time. We strive with every title to preserve the essential "living wisdom" of the author or artist. It is our goal to create products that not only provide information to a reader or listener, but that also embody the quality of a wisdom transmission.

For those seeking genuine transformation, Sounds True is your trusted partner. At SoundsTrue.com you will find a wealth of free resources to support your journey, including exclusive weekly audio interviews, free downloads, interactive learning tools, and other special savings on all our titles.

To learn more, please visit SoundsTrue.com/bonus/free_gifts or call us toll free at 800-333-9185.